VEGGIE & VEGAN
LONDON

A GUIDE TO ETHICAL EATING
IN THE CAPITAL

Veggie & Vegan London

Written by Edward Prendeville
Photographs by Andrew Kershman
Cover Photograph by Catherine Gratwicke, reproduced
by kind permission of www.redemptionbar.co.uk
Illustrations by Lesley Gilmour and Hannah Kershman
Book design by Susi Koch and Lesley Gilmour
Edited by Abigail Willis

Published in 2019 by
Metro Publications Ltd
PO Box 6336
London
N1 6PY

Printed and bound in China. This book is produced using
paper from registered sustainable and managed sources.

© 2018 Metro Publications Ltd
British Library Cataloguing in Publication Data.
A catalogue record for this book is available from the
British Library.

ISBN: 978-1-902910-62-8

VEGGIE & VEGAN
LONDON

A GUIDE TO ETHICAL EATING
IN THE CAPITAL

Edward Prendeville

Acknowledgements

I'd like to thank everyone at Metro Publications for their help and support in writing this book. Susi Koch and Andrew Kershman were there every step of the way, from designing its pages to providing support and guidance. Andrew also took on the Herculean task of doing all the photography; his images have helped bring the book to life. Lesley Gilmour deserves special mention; her expertly made maps have transformed my ramble of restaurants and shops into a user-friendly, area-coded guide. Our editor, Abigail Willis, has gone to a lot of trouble to save you, the reader, from tripping up over spelling mistakes and wayward grammar, and has turned the book into a far smoother read.

In the year it's taken to research and write this book, I have had the pleasure of visiting a great many vegan and vegetarian restaurants to taste and test what our capital's ethical kitchens are creating. Running an eatery is a difficult enterprise and it has been a joy to meet the chefs, taste their food and hear their stories. I've had great fun exploring vegan events and markets across the capital, such as London Fields Vegan Market and Vegan Nights. The organisers of these events have been hugely supportive of my work and the events themselves have been an inspiration. Lastly, my thanks go to all the veggies and vegans I have met on my travels whose generous support and recommendations have helped to make this book as comprehensive as it possibly can be.

Contents

Calthorpe Project

Introduction

I've lost track of the number of times a friend or family member has scoffed at the idea of vegetarianism and veganism. I remember often being presented with a single uninspiring vegan option when dining out that only reinforced these stereotypes. Rest assured things have changed for the better and while researching this book I have seen the number of meat-free eateries in London reach three figures and tasted delicious vegan and veggie dishes from across the globe.

With the explosion of meat-free cooking in the capital's kitchens, you'll be spoilt for choice for gourmet and casual eating options. Today you can try Ethiopian vegan stews from the likes of Engocha, indulgent vegan street food from Temple of Seitan as well as fine-dining experiences at up-market restaurants such as Farmacy. I've scoured the corners of our city for the start-ups, independents and local gems that populate the pages of this book and which have all been mapped out neighbourhood by neighbourhood, making your exploration of both your own back yard and uncharted territory all the more enjoyable. And of course, we've featured the 'institutions' of vegetarian and vegan cooking, such as Manna in Primrose Hill, which started as an alternative eatery in 1967 and is now one of London's smartest vegan restaurants.

The influx of plant-based businesses is not confined to restaurants. These days in the capital you can find clothes, household items and groceries all available from first-rate, sustainable and cruelty-free providers. There are new vegan markets opening all the time and events like Vegan Nights are transforming the plant-based social scene. You won't want to miss these on your travels, but with this book as your guide, there's no excuse not to live a little more vegetarian and vegan in London.

Edward Prendeville

LONDON TRANSPORT

The Spread Eagle

RESTAURANTS, CAFÉS & BARS

CENTRAL

Bloomsbury & Fitzrovia

Restaurants, Cafés & Bars:

1) Calthorpe Project
   Garden Café
2) Crosstown Doughnuts
3) Ethos
4) Ginger Jules Café
5) Kin Café
6) Mary Ward Café
7) Sagar
8) Thenga Café

Shops:

A) Alara Health Store, p.326
B) Planet Organic, p.328
C) Planet Organic, p.328

Calthorpe Project Garden Café ❶
HOMEMADE CAFÉ STAPLES
Calthorpe Project, Gray's Inn Road, WC1X 8LH
Tel: 020 7837 8019
www.calthorpeproject.org.uk
Twitter:@Calthorpepro
Travel: King's Cross LU
Open: Mon-Fri 10am-3pm

This small community project has so much on offer, it provides allotment spaces and workshops for the local community, the elderly and marginalised minority groups, as well as a café serving tasty veggie food. The produce often comes straight from the surrounding gardens. Toasties, vegetable mezze and soup are their staples, but you'll likely find Spanish omelette and pizza too. There are plenty of snacks, hot drinks and maybe some vegan cake, all reasonably priced for between £3 and £5.

The café is an eco-friendly business too –its biodegester turns food waste into biogas and fertiliser, which can then be used to cook and grow produce, keeping the environmental impact of its tasty food to a minimum. The seating spans from the café into the lush allotment space. A great place to escape the bustle of King's Cross and enjoy some greener food, Calthorpe Project Garden Café is a hidden veggie gem.

£
Vegetarian
Some Gluten Free

Branch

Crosstown Doughnuts ❷
Fitzrovia, 13 Newman Street, W1T 1PB
www.crosstowndoughnuts.com
Full review see page 46

Ethos ❸

INTERNATIONAL VEGETARIAN BUFFET

48 Eastcastle Street, W1W 8DX
Tel: 020 3581 1538
www.ethosfoods.com
Insta: @ethosfoods
Travel: Oxford Circus LU
Open: Mon-Fri 8am-10pm, Sat 11.30am-10pm, Sun 11am-5pm

Love it or loathe it, Oxford Street is London's busiest shopping street. You needn't traverse it for long, however, to find an eatery that pushes all the right buttons. Ethos boasts an eclectic mix of cuisines that rivals any establishment in the capital. Here you'll find bowls of sumptuously fleshy Japanese miso-roasted aubergines, golden chickpea and coconut curries, and the in-house special, Scotch eggs with oozing inners.

A pay-by-weight buffet service allows you to mix and match from over forty dishes for a culinary world tour. The breakfasts and desserts are not as regionally diverse, yet make up for this with abundant flavour and stylish presentation. The only thing better looking than the food might be the award-winning interior. Columns of silver birch make the space feel alive, and the seating and serving areas have a cool Scandinavian minimalist design. Ethos does a great job of showing that delicious food from anywhere can have a small footprint, with a menu that's always at least 50% vegan, gluten free, refined sugar free and minimises wastage. Despite the stylish interior and central London location, you can eat here inexpensively, with a generous plate of food usually priced between £5 and £10. In short, everything about Ethos makes it one of the top places to visit for vegans, veggies and 'flexies' alike in London.

£
Vegetarian
Some Gluten Free and Raw

Ginger Jules Café ❹
GARDEN KIOSK
Gordon Square, WC1H 0PD
Twitter: @GingerJulesCafé
Travel: Euston Square LU
Open: Mon-Fri 8.30am-4pm

Nestled among the trees in tranquil Gordon Square, you'll find this kiosk serving fantastic healthy and homely vegetarian and vegan food to be enjoyed sitting at their tables and chairs or while on the go. On offer are both snacks and meals, so whether you fancy soup and a sandwich, quiche or curry, or just a croissant and coffee, you need look no further. On warm days, look out for Jules' homemade sorbets which are a delicious way to cool down, particularly when enjoyed in the shade of this leafy Georgian square.

Everything here is great value, with homemade cakes and other snacks and drinks costing £2 or less, and hot meals for between £3 and £4. Ginger Jules is also committed to being an eco-friendly business, offering discounts to anyone bringing their own mugs/cups for drinks, and using biodegradable goods instead of plastic, which can be put in their composter and turned into soil for the small but healthy selection of plants that surround the hut. On fine days Ginger Jules is well worth seeking out and offers one of the best al fresco dining experiences in the capital, with delicious home cooked food at a price anyone can afford. A welcome change from the anonymous corporate caffs now found in many of central London's parks.

£
Vegetarian

Kin Café ❺

HOMEMADE CAFÉ STAPLES

22 Foley Street, W1W 6DT
Tel: 020 7998 4720
www.kincafe.co.uk
Insta: @kin_cafe
Travel: Goodge Street LU
Open: Mon-Fri 7.30am-5.30pm, Sat 10am-5pm

Kin stands out as an oasis of meat-free dining among a host of popular eateries in the salubrious Bloomsbury backstreets. It manages to balance being a friendly, family-run enterprise with loyal regulars, while boasting a trendy, sleek interior that is worthy of a special veggie & vegan breakfast or lunch trip.

Both the breakfast (7.30-11.30am) and lunch (11.30am-5/5.30pm) menus are rooted in seasonal dishes, so you'll find something new every time you visit. Lunch options include salads, sandwiches, soups and stews, alongside other great cooked and raw options, all of which are bursting with essential nutrients. The food and drink here is clearly prepared with care and love using delicious and healthy produce, so it really doesn't matter if you're popping in for a coffee or lining up to chow down on Burger Fridays, you're bound to enjoy the experience. There is indoor and outdoor seating, making this eatery equally suitable for visits on fine days. Breakfast dishes on average cost a reasonable £4-£7, and you'll only pay a little more for a substantial lunch. Kin gets no bad marks from us – it's a 5 star veggie and vegan spot.

£
Vegetarian
Some Gluten Free and Raw

Mary Ward Café ⑥

HOMEMADE ITALIAN

42 Queen Square, WC1N 3AQ

Tel: 020 7269 6085

www.marywardcentre.ac.uk/about/café

Travel: Russel Square LU

Open: Mon-Thurs 9.30am-8.45pm, Fri 9.30am-8pm, Sat 9.30am-4pm

Found within the Mary Ward Centre itself, this little café is popular with the staff, students and visitors alike, so much so that on occasion you'll find fast-flowing queues that extend beyond the door. Serving a daily rotating menu of vegetarian and vegan foods (with GF options too), the focus is split between fresh Italian dishes and hearty veggie baked dishes. The produce is unpretentious – here you'll find easy flavours and generous portions across the board. Prices match this ethos and you'll struggle to spend more than £5 per person for a filling lunch here. The space itself is small but inviting, with disabled access and interesting art adorning the walls, but if you don't fancy staying then takeout is available and Queen's Square Gardens across the road is a pleasant place to enjoy your food. The Mary Ward Café is great for a full meal or as somewhere to go for a slice of vegan cake and coffee, so if you're in the area and looking for somewhere inexpensive, it's definitely worth a visit.

£

Some Gluten Free
Vegetarian & Vegan

Branch

Sagar ⑦

SOUTH INDIAN

17a Percy Street, W1T 1DU

Tel: 020 7631 3319

www.sagarveg.co.uk

Full review see page 40

Thenga Café ❽
VEGETARIAN THALIS
120 Cromer Street, WC1H 8BS
Tel: 020 3817 9919
www.thengacafe.com
Insta: @thengacafekx
Travel: King's Cross LU
Open: Mon–Thurs 10am-6pm, Fri 10am-4pm

You could walk past the brick walls of 120 Cromer Street without ever realising what lay behind them, unless you were lucky enough to spot the blackboard outside advertising Thenga Café. Inside, the modest canteen environment of the place doesn't do justice to the special food and service you'll find here. The building itself is split between being a yoga studio and eatery, with the latter offering a good selection of organic hot and cold drinks and vegetarian baked goods throughout the day.

Their speciality, however, is the daily rotating vegan curries, served in the classic steel tray style (where you get a variety of curries alongside rice and usually roti). Thenga will give you a taste of authentic Indian food, a rare find among the proliferation of anglicised Indian restaurants. Expect great service from the friendly staff as you relax for lunch in the café's high ceilinged and quirkily decorated space. Thenga is popular with the local student community with curries for just £5-£6, and organic coffees and juices for around £2. Thenga is a great option for a budget vegetarian meal in the capital and one heartily recommended.

£
Vegetarian
Vegan

Vanilla Black

The City

Restaurants, Cafés & Bars:

1) Falafel House (Cannon Street)
2) Falafel House (Carter Lane)
3) Pilpel Fleet Street
4) Pilpel St Paul's
5) Pilpel Lime Street
6) Vanilla Black

FARRINGDON

BARBICAN

Bunhill
Fields

CHISWELL ST

BEECH ST

CROSS ST

ALDERSGATE ST

SILK ST

ROPEMAKER ST

CHARTERHOUSE ST

Smithfield
Market

CHANCERY
LANE

FARRINGDON RD

Barbican

MOORGATE

FURNIVAL ST

FETTER LANE

HATTON GDNS

LEATHER LANE

LITTLE
BRITAIN

FORE ST

LONDON WALL

HOLBORN VIADUCT

Museum
of London

LONDON WALL

LONDON WALL

6

NEWGATE ST

LOTHBURY

MOORGATE

CHANCERY LANE

CITY
THAMESLINK

ST PAUL'S

4

L. GRESHAM ST

THREADNEEDLE ST

3

CITY
THAMESLINK

PATERNOSTER SQ

CHEAPSIDE

KING ST

BANK

CORNHILL

FLEET ST

FETTER LANE

2

LUDGATE HILL

St Paul's

NEW CHANGE

LOMBARD ST

5

WHITEFRIARS ST

FLEET LANE

MANSION
HOUSE

QUEEN VICTORIA ST

GRACECHURCH ST

NEW BRIDGE ST

QUEEN VICTORIA ST

CANNON ST

MONUMENT

MIDDLE TEMPLE LANE

Inner Temple
Gardens

UPPER THAMES ST

CANNON
STREET

1

VICTORIA EMBANKMENT

BLACKFRIARS

BLACKFRIARS
BRIDGE

MILLENNIUM
BRIDGE

SOUTHWARK
BRIDGE

LONDON
BRIDGE

Thames Path

Tate Modern

STONEY ST

Falafel House
FALAFEL

1

116 Cannon Street, EC4N 6AS
Tel: 020 7626 6570
www.falafel-house.co.uk
Travel: Monument LU
Open: Mon-Fri 10am-4pm

2

48 Carter Lane, EC4V 5EA
Tel: 020 7248 3228
www.falafel-house.co.uk
Travel: St Paul's LU
Open: Mon-Fri 10am-4pm

This easy-going chain of falafel eateries can get very busy during lunch service, as it caters to the vast workforce of the City's financial area. It has a reputation for plentiful portions and perfect pittas and fillings, all for not too much money and easy to eat on the go. Pitta, salad and falafel can be enjoyed for under a fiver, and you only need to pay a quid or two extra to load up with some sides like grilled aubergine, feta cheese or guacamole. There is limited seating in both branches, but with no nonsense service and little in the way of décor, Falafel House is ideal for a tasty takeaway lunch that doesn't break the bank.

£
Vegetarian

Pilpel

FALAFEL
www.pilpel.co.uk
Insta: @pilpelforthepeople

3 Fleet Street
146 Fleet Street, 1a Wine Office Court, EC4M 3BY
Tel: 020 7952 1205
Tube: Blackfriars LU
Open: Mon-Fri 11am-4pm

4 St Paul's
Unit 5, Queen's Head Passage, Paternoster Square, EC4M 7DZ
Tel: 020 7248 9281
Tube: St. Paul's LU
Open: Mon-Fri 10am-9pm

5 Lime Street
21 Lime Street, EC3V 1PL
Tel: 020 7199 2969
Tube: Monument LU
Open: Mon-Fri 10am-8pm

Pilpel is a 100% vegetarian chain of Israeli eateries, and a
real gem. It is only found within the parameters of the City
of London and has thrived catering for the large numbers of
white-collar workers looking for a quick, good quality lunch.
The success of Pilpel stems from its traditionally inspired falafel
and houmous dishes, served fresh from the pan alongside
great vegetable salads and pittas. We love this no-nonsense
approach to grub and recommend their falafel and pitta with
a bit of extra aubergine and lots of salad. There's plenty of
seating but during lunch hour you're likely to be surrounded
by a horde of eager fellow diners. If you fancy a takeaway the
falafel sandwich is the perfect food to eat on the go. The service

is remarkably quick even at busy times and they don't mess around with their prices either – £5 for a hearty lunch is great value for the City of London. Strongly recommended.

Branches:
Aldgate, 60 Alie Street, E1 8PX (see p. 315)
Old Spitalfields Market, Pavillion Building, E1 6EW (see p. 300)
Spitalfields, 38 Brushfield Street, E1 6AT (see p. 301)

£
Vegetarian
Some Gluten Free

Vanilla Black ❻

INTERNATIONAL FINE DINING

Chancery Lane, 17-18 Took's Court, EC4A 1LB
Tel: 020 7242 2622
www.vanillablack.co.uk
Twitter: @vanillablack1/Insta: @vanilla_black_uk
Travel: Chancery Lane LU
Open: Mon-Sat 12noon-2.30pm & 6pm-10pm

Vanilla Black exists as an antidote to London's meat-centric restaurant culture, offering a unique vegetarian take on the fine dining experience. The restaurant is situated among the bustle of the City's financial district, but offers welcome respite from the relentless outside. The space is sleek, with dark wood furnishing, tasteful lighting and polished décor. But this is really an accompaniment to the excellent meat-free menu.

A la carte (2 or 3 courses), 5 course tasting and set lunch menus are available, spanning all manner of culinary fusions. Beige and bland are off the table, so don't shy away from trying mushroom fudge, cucumber ketchup or a seaweed broth and quail egg combo. Soft drinks and mocktails are available, but opening a bottle of vintage wouldn't be unwarranted. Most dishes can be cooked for vegans and the wheat intolerant and this is definitely a restaurant to challenge a carnivore's expectations of cruelty-free cooking. Booking in advance is advisable, as is setting aside some change. Lunch starts at £21 per head, and dinner ranges between £31 and £55 depending on the number of courses. Wine is available by the glass or the bottle, with the latter starting at £25. The prices might be high, but for a special occasion there are few restaurants that can match Vanilla Black.

£££££
Vegetarian
Some Gluten Free

The Gate Islington

Clerkenwell & Old Street

Restaurants, Cafés & Bars:

1) Arancini Brothers
2) The Blacksmith & The Toffeemaker
3) Carnevale
4) The Gate Islington
5) Veggie Pret

Arancini Brothers ❶
RISOTTO BALLS & FAST FOOD
42 Old St, London EC1V 9AE
www.arancinibrothers.com
Full review see page 69

The Blacksmith & the Toffeemaker ❷
VEGAN GASTROPUB
292-294 St John Street, EC1V 4PA
www.theblacksmithandthetoffeemaker.co.uk
Twitter:@TB_and_TT
Insta: @blacksmith_and_toffeemaker
Travel: Angel/Farringdon LU
Open: Mon-Sat 12noon-3pm & 5pm-10pm, Sun Closed
This charming local pub is a good place to enjoy a drink but
they now offer some great vegan grub too. The homely, informal
atmosphere lends itself to a casual evening out, where you
can enjoy burgers and other easy-going British pub foods like
mac & cheese, or bread & butter pudding, alongside a host of
beverages on tap. The prices are reasonable with everything
on the menu under £10. The B&T have gone above and beyond
the expectations of a vegan business in using recyclable and
biodegradable products wherever possible, and for committing
to sustainable water and food wastage practices. The interior
is a trendy fusion between modern industrial and classic British
features, and there are plenty of seats, whether you've come for
food, drink or the weekly pub quiz. Feel free to bring along your
pooch, and make a day or evening out of it. A great vegan pub.

£
Vegan
Some Gluten Free

Clerkenwell & Old Street

Boost your meals with nutrients and antioxidants. One teaspoon of the powder is equal to a handful of fresh, wildly grown Arctic berries, which can have up to three times the nutrients of cultivated berries.

See all the London stockists or shop at

www.arcticpowerberries.com

Carnevale ❸
MEDITERRANEAN
135 Whitecross Street, EC1Y 8JL
Tel: 020 7250 3452
www.carnevalerestaurant.co.uk
Travel: Barbican LU
Open: Mon-Fri 12noon-3pm & 5pm-11pm, Sat 5-11pm
Carnevale is a long-established, friendly local restaurant on
Whitecross Street, just a stone's throw from the Barbican. It
serves vegetarian dishes inspired from all of the Mediterranean's
varying regional cuisines. Here you can enjoy falafel and
tabbouleh or gnocchi and ravioli and they also have vegan and
gluten free options. The prices reflect the area and Carnevale's
commitment to fine dining using quality ingredients. The interior
is plainly furnished and there's a semi al fresco seating area too.
They also have a delivery service, and a street food market stall
called Saladin that sells their range of dishes at the midweek
Whitecross Street market, for those needing lunch on the go.
Carnevale is a simple vegetarian restaurant serving healthy,
tasty and meat-free Mediterranean food and a great option for a
meat-free special occasion.

££
Vegetarian
Some Gluten Free
Some Vegan

Branch

The Gate Islington ❹
INTERNATIONAL FINE DINING
370 St John Street, Clerkenwell, EC1V 4NN
Tel: 020 7278 5483
www.thegaterestaurants.com
Full review see page 148

BRANCH

Veggie Pret ❺
VEGGIE ONLY SANDWICH SHOP
21 Exmouth Market, EC1R 4QD
www.pret.co.uk
Full review see page 60

The Gate Islington

by Chloe

Covent Garden

Restaurants, Cafés & Bars:

1) by Chloe
2) Poetry Society
3) Sagar
4) Wild Food Café

Shops:

A) Neal's Yard Remedies, p.328
B) Ena Salon, p.350

HOLBORN

TOTTENHAM
COURT ROAD

NEW OXFORD ST

HIGH HOLBORN

PARKER ST

B

KINGSWAY

CHARING CROSS RD

SHAFTESBURY AVE

ENDELL ST

SHORTS GDNS

BETTERTON ST

2

GREAT QUEEN ST

DRURY LANE

A

4

NEAL ST

ST

EARLHAM

SHELTON ST

LONG ACRE

BOW ST

1

RUSSELL ST

3

WELLINGTON ST

ALDWYCH

WEST ST

MONMOUTH ST

Royal Opera
House

SHAFTESBURY AVE

COVENT
GARDEN

JAMES ST

Apple
Market

TAVISTOCK ST

LISLE ST

LEICESTER
SQUARE

ST MARTIN'S LANE

KING ST

BEDFORD ST

STRAND

STRAND

LEICESTER
SQUARE

IRVINE ST

CHANDOS PL

WHITCOMB ST

National
Gallery

CHARING
CROSS ROAD

TRAFALGAR SQ

COCKSPUR ST

35

by Chloe ❶
INTERNATIONAL
Drury House, 34-43 Russell Street, WC2B 5HA
Tel: 020 388 33273
www.eatbychloe.com
Twitter/Insta: @eatbychloe
Travel: Covent Garden LU
Open: Daily 10am-11pm

This popular US export from the vegan celeb chef Chloe Coscarelli has washed up on our shores, with two central London branches under its belt so far. The stores are super spacious, with creative décor, lighting and hanging chairs that make for pleasant places to enjoy some good plant-based food. There's a lot to choose from on a menu that includes British classics like Fish'n'Chips and Sticky Toffee Pudding, as well as salads, burgers and brunch staples. Rather than follow the clean eating fad, byChloe offers food that feels indulgent, but without too much junk. The portions however, aren't large for the price with £9 for a bite-size guac burger a little on the high side. Despite the New York prices, byChloe is still a reputable option when on a cruelty-free culinary trip to the capital. Check out their creative, colour-coded Instagram to get a feel for what this vegan brand is all about.

Branch:
Tower Bridge, One Tower Bridge, Duchess Walk, SE1 2SH, see page 232

££
Vegan
Some Gluten Free

Poetry Society ❷
VEGETARIAN CAFÉ AND PERFORMANCE VENUE
22 Betterton Street, WC2H 9BX
Tel: 020 7420 9888;
www.poetrysociety.org.uk
Travel: Covent Garden LU
Open: Mon-Fri 11am till late & some Saturdays

The Poetry Society and Café is one London's more unusual eating spots, in that you can enjoy something from their vegetarian menu while taking part in poetry recitals, workshops and open mic sessions. Hidden down a quiet street in Covent Garden, here you can escape from the surrounding rush and relax. You'll find a small menu that features soups, mezze and sandwiches, as well as a vegan option or two and all the standard baked café goods. They've also sourced some of their hot and soft drinks from local fairtrade suppliers.

It's an inviting space with regular events to take advantage of if you like poetry. There are plenty of tables and chairs to sit at while you peruse the books they have lining the walls, and posters detail all the events to look forward to. Prices are fair, with meals costing between £5 and £7, and all drinks and pastries for under £3. The Poetry Society has a good deal of charm, and is a great place to find good food and hopefully some poetic inspiration. Make sure to check out what they've got on when you're next in this neck of the woods.

£
Vegetarian

Sagar ❸
SOUTH INDIAN

31 Catherine Street, WC2B 5JS
Tel: 020 7836 6377
www.sagarveg.co.uk
Travel: Covent Garden LU
Open: Mon-Sat 12noon-11pm, Sun 12noon-10pm

Sagar is a successful South Indian restaurant chain, with branches across Central and West London. They specialise in Thalis (mixed curry platter on a steel tray, alongside rice and bread), using tropical fruits that are typical of South Indian cuisine. Mango, lime and especially coconut are the basis of their flavours, and dishes are primarily based on lentils. Kootu – a creamy, nutty curry – is always a safe option for the spice averse, but the emphasis here is on good flavour and texture without excessive heat.

Sagar also has a nice selection of traditional sweet things to try, from your standard Kulfis to less commonly found fried milk dumplings. The restaurants themselves are all pleasant places to relax and enjoy your meal. Prices are reasonable – expect to spend £20 a head (including drinks) for a comprehensive meal. Offering friendly service and a traditional menu that has remained consistently good over the years, Sagar is a great place for authentic southern Indian cuisine.

Branches:
Hammersmith, 157 King Street, W6 9JT, see page 149
Harrow, 57 Station Road, HA2 7SR, see page 321
Fitzrovia, 17a Percy Street, W1T 1DU, see page 17

£££
Vegetarian

Wild Food Café ❹
ORGANIC WHOLEFOODS CAFÉ

1st Floor, 14 Neal's Yard, WC2H 9D
Tel: 020 7419 2014
www.wildfoodcafe.com
Travel: Covent Garden LU
Open: Tues-Thurs 11.30am-8pm, Fri-Sat 11.30am-9pm,
Sun 11.30am-6pm

On the first floor of a charming, wisteria adorned building, tucked away in a Covent Garden courtyard is the always busy Wild Food Café. This is a vegan eatery whose mantra is to serve raw and wholefood dishes using ingredients sourced from the best local suppliers. You won't find refined sugars, gluten or over-processed ingredients like wheat and peanuts anywhere on their fantastic seasonal menu. Instead the offer here is well thought through and carefully prepared. Expect super food ingredients like probiotic kimchi and wild nettle featuring in a great selection of bowls, salads and sandwiches. The dessert menu is equally daring with sweet potato brownies and hibiscus cheesecake.

Daily specials mean you won't run out of things to try on repeat visits. Considering the communal seating and casual atmosphere, paying £20 for a full meal here can feel expensive. You will however be supporting a venture that shares the values and ethos of Neal's Yard, a hub of alternative London for 40 years. The place might get busy but there is always a friendly and welcoming atmosphere, making this a great café to visit when in the centre of town.

£££
Vegan
Some Gluten Free and Raw

Marylebone & Mayfair

Restaurants, Cafés & Bars:

1) Crosstown Doughnuts, Piccadilly
2) Crosstown Doughnuts, Picton Place
3) Deliciously Ella
4) The Gate Marylebone
5) Tibits
6) Woodlands Marylebone

Shops:

A) Stella McCartney, p.335

Crosstown Doughnuts
DOUGHNUTS AND DRINKS

35 Piccadilly, W1J 0DW ❶
Tel: 020 7287 7671
Open: Mon-Thurs 8am-10pm,
Fri 8am-11pm, Sat 9am-11pm,
Sun 9am-8pm

5-6 Picton Place, W1U 1BL ❷
Tel: 020 7487 3733
Open: Mon-Fri 9am-6pm,
Sat-Sun 10am-6.30pm

www.crosstowndoughnuts.com
Twitter/Insta: @crosstowndough/crosstowndoughnuts
Travel: Bond Street LU

This chain of doughnut and coffee shops has a vegan branch in Marylebone, a vegan stall at Brockley Market, and also stocks 10 or so varieties of vegan doughnuts in their other stores around London. A glance at their Instagram is likely to seal the deal, as these doughnuts aren't limited to the dull sugar-dusted varieties in the supermarkets. Instead, think multi-coloured glazes, oozing homemade jams and custards and crumbled toppings aplenty. Using a mixture of plant-based alternatives like chia seeds, coconut butter, mylks, and tofu, they've achieved vegan doughnuts that really rival their dairy doppelgängers. You can enjoy a range of drinks alongside them, including Kombucha, chocolate milks and coffee from the Caravan Roastery. Their 'premium' doughnuts will set you back £3.50, but Crosstown's goodies are a fun way to enjoy a vegan treat.

£
Vegan

Branches:
Soho, 4 Broadwick Street, W1F 0DA, see page 54
Fitzrovia, 13 Newman Street, W1T 1PB, see page 9
Shoreditch, 157 Brick Lane, E1 6SB, see page 293

Deliciously Ella ❸

INTERNATIONAL GLUTEN-FREE

18-20 Weighhouse Street, W1K 5LU
www.deliciouslyella.com
Insta: @deliciouslyella
Travel: Bond Street LU
Open: Mon–Fri 7.30am-7pm, Sat–Sun 9am-7pm

Deliciously Ella was opened by Ella Mills, the cookery author and entrepreneur who founded Deliciously Ella, in a joint venture with her husband and business partner. They've successfully brought the plant-based philosophy of Deliciously Ella to life in this physical store. Open all day, it serves breakfast and lunches, with the former tending to lean on the sweet stuff, like fruity porridges, pancakes and puddings, and the latter featuring dishes from around the world. You can expect to enjoy arrays of salads, falafels and tagines, as well as a variety of chillies and curries. These are reasonably priced, especially considering the average price point in the area and of other 'health food' alternatives. Breakfasts cost between £5 and £6, and most mains between £8 and £9. Fittingly, the interior is an Instagrammer's delight – Scandinavian minimalist décor, plenty of natural light and rustic wooden tables will help you get that perfect picture.

£-££
Vegan
Gluten Free

Branch

The Gate Marylebone ❹
INTERNATIONAL FINE DINING
22-24 Seymour Pl, Marylebone, W1H 7NL
Tel: 020 7724 6656
www.thegaterestaurants.com
see review on page 148

Branch

Tibits ❺
INTERNATIONAL VEGETARIAN BUFFET
12-14 Heddon Street W1B 4DA
Tel: 020 7758 4112
www.tibits.co.uk
See review on page 232

The Gate

Woodlands Marylebone ⑥

SOUTH INDIAN

77 Marylebone Lane, W1U 2PS
Tel: 020 7486 3862
www.woodlandsrestaurant.co.uk
Travel: Bond Street LU
Open: Mon-Fri 12noon-2.45pm & 6pm-10.45pm,
Sat-Sun 12noon-10.45pm

Woodlands is a chain restaurant with a rich history of serving vegetarian, pan-Indian cuisine both back home and across London. Having catered to meat-free curry needs since the '80s they specialise in South Indian dishes, and also offer vegan and Jain options. Though they have attempted 'modernising' both the restaurant's food and interior, they still offer standard Indian fare with few surprises.

Expect big portions of oil rich Dosa and curry platters that can be washed down with sweet lassis. You don't need to worry about bringing a bottle – they serve classic Cobra and Kingfisher beers, as well as a range of organic wines. Woodlands' prices reflect their branches' salubrious locations, with meals likely to cost over £20 per head, but they are a reliable place to enjoy Indian vegetarian cuisine while out in town.

Branches:
Piccadilly, 37 Panton Street, SW1Y 4EA, see p.61
Hampstead, 102 Heath Street, NW3 1DR , see p.96

£££
Vegetarian
Vegan

Norman's Coach and Horses

Soho

Restaurants, Cafés & Bars:

1) Crosstown Doughnuts, Soho
2) Govinda's
3) Mildred's
4) Norman's Coach and Horses
5) Veggie Pret
6) Woodlands Piccadilly
7) YORICA!

Shops:

OXFORD CIRCUS

OXFORD ST

NOEL ST

GREAT MARLBOROUGH ST

D'ARBLAY ST

POLAND ST

BROADWICK ST

MARSHALL ST

CARNABY ST

KINGLY ST

BEAK ST

GOLDEN SQUARE

BRIDLE LANE

LEXINGTON ST

BRIDGE ST

WARDOUR ST

BROADWICK ST

BREWER ST

WARWICK ST

REGENT ST

GLASSHOUSE ST

DENMAN ST

PICCADILLY CIRCUS

COVENTRY ST

HAY MARKET

PANTON ST

SHAFTESBURY AVENUE

PETER ST

DEAN ST

SO HO SQUARE

FRITH ST

GREEK ST

OLD COMPTON ST

ROM ILLY ST

MANETTE ST

CARING CROSS RD.

TOTTENHAM COURT ROAD

GERARD ST

LISLE ST

LEICESTER SQUARE

LEICESTER SQUARE

53

Crosstown Doughnuts Soho ❶
4 Broadwick Street, W1F 0DA
www.crosstowndoughnuts.com
See review on page 46

Govinda's ❷
INDIAN
10 Soho Street, W1D 3D
Tel: 020 7437 3662
Travel: Tottenham Court LU
Open: Mon-Sat 12noon-9pm, Sun 12noon-4.30pm

Govinda's is a vegetarian restaurant situated on the ground floor of the Radha Krishna Temple between Soho Square and Oxford Street. Their speciality is 'Thali', a style of curry platters where you mix and match smaller portions of different dishes along with rice and bread. They also claim that all their food is karma free – not least because it doesn't contain meat or eggs – but also because their food is offered to Lord Krishna before being served, which is known as a 'prasadam', meaning blessed with the god's mercy.

Here you can expect mixed vegetable curries, chutneys and dahls that are easy on the palate and your wallet (£10 gets you unlimited servings). They also offer non-Indian foods like pastas and quiches but their Indian foods are definitely the better option. Food is served within an unpretentious, canteen style interior. Govinda's is popular with anyone looking for cheap and cheerful Indian grub whether you follow Hare Krishna or just like the atmosphere of the place. Govinda's is a real London institution and one well worth seeking out.

£
Vegetarian

Mildred's Soho ③
INTERNATIONAL
45 Lexington Street, W1F 9AN
Tel: 020 7494 1634
www.mildreds.co.uk
Insta: @mildredsrestaurants
Travel: Oxford Circus LU
Open: Mon-Sat 12noon-11pm

Mildred's first opened its doors in 1988 when being vegetarian was considered an eccentric fad. They have always challenged the idea that vegetarianism was about 'brown mush served in earthenware bowls', instead offering attractive and delicious food from across the world. You can expect to enjoy burritos and burgers alongside South East Asian curries and broths, and many more dishes borrowed from global cuisine. This can all be enjoyed alongside a grown-up selection of drinks, with plenty of organic wines and cocktails to choose from, making Mildred's feel like a far cry from the dull stereotypes of vegetarianism.

Like a growing number of restaurants, they don't take bookings, which can involve a wait for a table during peak times. If you're willing to hang about or are fortunate enough to beat the queues, then you can enjoy accessible vegan and vegetarian food inside a casual, modern dining space that makes for a pleasant evening for devout vegetarians, vegans and curious omnivores alike. Prices are a little more upmarket for what you get when compared to their competition, with mains fixed at £12 and smaller plates/sides for £5-£8, but their success in opening multiple branches across the capital is a testament to the continued faith in the Mildred's ethos. One of the longest and most successful plant-focused food establishments in town, Mildred's has a deservedly loyal following.

Branches:
Mildred's King's Cross, 200 Pentonville Rd, N1 9JP, see page 122
Mildred's Camden, 9 Jamestown Rd, NW1 7BW, see page 82
Mildred's Dalston, 1 Dalston Square, E8 3GU, see page 262

££
Vegetarian
Some Gluten Free

Norman's Coach and Horses ❹

TRADITIONAL BRITISH PUB
29 Greek Street, W1D 5DH
Tel: 020 7437 5920
www.coachsoho.co.uk
Twitter: @CoachSoho
Travel: Tottenham Court Road LU
Open: Mon-Sat 12noon-10pm, Sun 12noon-8pm

The legendary pub landlord, Norman Balon, has long departed along with some of his more famous regulars, but the pub which bears his name endures as a Soho institution. The Coach and Horses continues to thrive and has remained largely the same while Soho changes by the day. The pub on the ground floor is still as Norman would remember it but upstairs there is now a dining room specialising in vegetarian food. Set out like a British tearoom during the day, this space doubles as the dining area by night and is well worth a visit.

Expect hearty servings of meat-free pie and mash or the equally popular 'Tofish and Chips' that uses seaweed to give a taste of the sea. Their 'Vedgeree' is our favourite fishless take on a classic. For Soho, the prices are as comforting as the food, and you'll be hard pressed to find as filling a meal for around £10 elsewhere in this part of town. Norman's is a treat for those wanting to enjoy a cuisine often off-limits to veggies and vegans. It's not gourmet or gastro – the dingy charm and history is what sustains this pub's loyal following and attracts new visitors keen to experience one of central London's last traditional boozers. Go for veggie and vegan twists on British food, wash it down with a pint and don't forget to raise a glass in memory of the irrascible Norman, London's erstwhile rudest landlord.

£-££
Vegetarian

Veggie Pret ⑤
VEGGIE ONLY SANDWICH SHOP
35 Broadwick Street, W1F 0DH
Tel: 020 7932 5274
www.pret.co.uk
Insta: @pretamangeruk
Travel: Oxford Circus LU
Open: Mon-Fri 6.30am-9.00pm, Sat 8am-8pm, Sun 9.30am-7pm

Amid the boom of plant-based eating in recent years, Pret A Manger emerged as a game changer being one of the first corporate giants to make a real commitment to vegetarian and vegan food. Veggie Pret has been so successful that it now has three branches and has plans for further expansion. You'll find a generous array of veggie and vegan ready to eat foods like sandwiches, salads and finger bites, as well as cold and hot drinks, all of which are designed to be enjoyed on the go but can be also eaten on site. The company uses mostly natural ingredients in their produce and anything left unsold at the end of the day is donated to charities combatting food poverty. They're also making a concerted effort to eliminate their use of plastic in packaging. Slightly more expensive than supermarket equivalents, Veggie Pret is still among the cheapest veggie and vegan food in London, with nearly everything costing less than £5 and plenty for less than £3. Veggie Pret is not only a good option for getting food while on the go in London, but also marks an important shift in our eating habits.

£
Vegetarian

Branches :
21 Exmouth Market, EC1R 4QD, see p.33
57 Great Eastern Street, EC2A 3QD, see p.305

Branch

Woodlands Piccadilly ❻
SOUTH INDIAN
37 Panton Street, SW1Y 4EA
www.woodlandsrestaurant.co.uk
See review on page 51

YORICA! ❼
VEGAN ICE CREAM PARLOUR
130 Wardour Street, W1F 8ZN
Tel: 020 7434 4370
www.yorica.com
Insta: @yoricamoments
Travel: Tottenham Court Road LU
Open: Mon-Weds 1pm-10pm, Thurs 11am-11pm,
Fri-Sat 11am-12midnight, Sun 12noon-10pm

Yorica! offers a chilled alternative to the frenetic activity of Wardour Street in Soho. London's only strictly vegan fro-yo and ice cream parlour, they offer a large array of flavours, tonnes of toppings as well as hot options of waffles & crepes. These desserts are definitely indulgent, featuring flavours like rainbow candy and gooey vanilla brownie and toppings that range from Jammy Dodgers to pomegranate hearts. We're keenest on their sharing tub of 'Mellow Matcha' fro-yo, with generous amounts of popping candy sprinkled over, as an intriguing and flavoursome way of satisfying your sugar cravings.

Inside the parlour is fun and inviting, but despite this atmosphere, the limited seating makes it harder to enjoy the warm woodlined and prettily decorated interior – it's definitely more of a 'to-go' establishment, which is what you'd expect really from an ice cream shop. It's expensive for what it is - £4-£6 only gets you the ice cream or fro-yo, and these are really best enjoyed with toppings that'll cost you more. Having said that, for those averse to dairy this is one of the only spots that'll properly cater to your ice cream needs. If you're passing and want something sweet, Yorica! is great option.

£
Vegan
Gluten Free

CLASSIC V CHEESEBURGER

£7.00

...r with a slice of mature cheddar vegan cheese,
...m bun with salad leaves, slow roasted tomato
...ickles, onion and creamy burger sauce.

...h barley, tomato concentrate, parsley, **soy sauce**, **miso**, herbs
...ushrooms, **wheat**, vegan mayo, **mustard**, **gluten**

CLASSIC V FACON CHEESEBURGER

our classic burger with strips of crispy maple facon, a slice of mature cheddar vegan
cheese, served on a warm bun with salad leaves, slow roasted tomato relish, pickles,
onion and creamy burger sauce.

£7.50

Ingredients: **British barley**, tomato concentrate, parsley, **soy sauce**, **miso**, herbs,
mushrooms, **wheat**, vegan mayo, **mustard**, **gluten**

VEGAN

THE HOLY SMOKE

our classic burger with a slice of smoked vegan cheese, served on a warm bun with BBQ sauce, smokey chipotle mayo & grilled onions.

£7.50

Ingredients **British barley**, tomato concentrate, parsley, **soy sauce**, **miso**, herbs, mushrooms, **wheat**, vegan mayo, **mustard**, **gluten**

NORTH

Camden, Kentish Town & Primrose Hill

Restaurants, Cafés & Bars:

1) Arancini Brothers
2) Club Mexicana
3) Dou Dou
4) The Fields Beneath
5) Hawraman Café
6) Magic Falafel
7) Manna
8) Mildred's Camden
9) Nectar Café
10) Purezza

11) Rudy's Dirty Vegan Diner
12) Square Root Camden
13) Temple of Camden
14) VBurger
15) What the Pitta!
16) Young Vegans

Shops:

A) Earth Natural Foods, p.344

KENTISH
TOWN

BELSIZE
PARK

HAVERSTOCK HILL

MAITLAND PARK VILLAS

QUEEN'S CRES

BASSET ST

MALDEN RD

GRAFTON RD

HOLMES RD

ISLIP ST

CAVERSHAM RD

GAISFORD ST **A**

PATSHULL RD

KENTISH TOWN RD

KENTISH
TOWN WEST **4**

PRINCE OF WALES RD

ROCHESTER RD

ETON RD

CHALK
FARM

CHALK FARM RD

ADELAIDE RD

HARMOOD ST

HARTLAND RD

CASTLE HAVEN RD

HAWLEY RD

1

CAMDEN
ROAD

KING HENRY'S RD

PRIMROSE HILL RD

AINGER RD

GLOUCESTER AVE

FITZROY RD

REGENT'S PARK RD

7

5

11
6
16 **14**
12 **2**

Camden
Market

Regent's Canal

JAMESTOWN RD

9

OVAL RD

INVERNESS ST

8

CAMDEN
TOWN

3

CAMDEN RD

KENTISH TOWN RD

ROYAL COLLEGE ST

BAYHAM ST

15

PARKWAY

ALBERT RD

10

ARLINGTON RD

CAMDEN HIGH RD

PRATT ST

13 →

DELANCEY ST

MORNINGTON
CRESCENT

REGENT'S
PARK

OUTER CIRCLE

ALBANY ST

PARK VILLAGE EAST

Arancini Brothers ❶
RISOTTO BALLS & FAST FOOD
115a Kentish Town Road, NW1 8PB
Twitter: @AranciniBros/Insta: @arancinibros
www.arancinibrothers.com
Travel: Camden Town LU
Open: Mon-Fri 8am-9.30pm, Sat-Sun 9.30am-9.30pm

After finding the perfect recipe for arancini balls on their travels, the duo of Dave's behind this flourishing vegan restaurant chain has taken London by storm. With three branches across the capital – in the hubs of Dalston, Old Street and Kentish Town – and a strong presence on the street food market scene, there are plenty of opportunities to try their deep fried risotto balls. Whether you want them by themselves, wrapped up tortilla style or wedged between a burger bun, these are a tasty healthy snack to enjoy on the go or in their casually styled café diners. For those looking for more of a meal, the Brothers do salad boxes, chips and veggie stews, as well as some soft drinks and sweet treats. Depending on the fillings and flavours you choose for your meal, prices vary from £5 to £10, which doesn't include sides. It's a tad more expensive than your typical street eatery, but well worth tucking into when in need of some substantial vegan grub.

Branches:

592 Kingsland Road, E8 4AH; (see page 257)
42 Old Street, EC1V 9AE; (see page 30)

££
Vegan
Some Gluten Free

Club Mexicana ❷
MEXICAN STREET FOOD
Unit 215-216, Camden Lock Market
Chalk Farm Road, NW1 8AB
www.clubmexicana.com
Insta: @clubmexicana
Travel: Camden Town LU
Open: Mon-Thurs 11am-6pm, Fri-Sun 11am-7pm

A shining example of how veganism and street food are taking the culinary world by storm right now is Club Mexicana. This 100% vegan Mexican street food eatery started as a single market stall in Camden Lock and has since expanded into catering for Shoreditch's Dinerama and The Spread Eagle – that's London's first vegan pub for the uninitiated. You might feel spoilt for choice by Camden's panoply of vegan and veggie stores and stalls, but the simplicity of Club Mexicana's formula makes it a contender for the top spot. Burritos, tacos, nachos – those staples we know so well - are the options on the menu here. Fantastic fillings of 'cheezy' beans, tofish or jackfruit keep these tasting authentic but meat-free (as Mexican cuisine typically isn't), and you needn't worry about missing out on guacamole or salsa, which are slathered all over the place.

The colours are vibrant, portions hearty and the constant queues testify to the popularity of this vegan take on Mexican street food. It's expensive as street food goes, costing at least £7 per person for a market stall meal, but we still think it's worth it for a tasty on the go lunch. Perfect paired with a soda or beer, it's no wonder that the vegan crowd go loco for Club Mexicana.

£
Vegan

Dou Dou ❸
THAI AND CHINESE BUFFET
6 Kentish Town Road, NW1 9NX
Tel: 077 1348 0552
Travel: Camden Town LU
Open: Mon-Fri 12noon-10:30pm, Sat-Sun 12noon-11pm

It's not an entirely meat-free nirvana in Camden, as is made evident by the sign alerting passers by to the KFC a 30 second walk away. For those looking for an alternative to fried chicken here, Dou Dou is a sound option. They are a vegan all-you-can-eat buffet serving a mish-mash of staple Chinese and Thai dishes with plenty of convincing meat substitutes. Expect to find sweet and sour 'chicken', 'beef' curries and 'prawn' noodles among a plethora of choice, including starters, desserts and some odd finds like boiled broccoli and roast potatoes.

The food on offer here unfortunately lives up to the MSG stereotype associated with South East Asian eateries – everything tastes rather glazed. Still, the convenience of the location coupled with the low prices – £5.90 or £6.90 for an unlimited lunch or dinner/weekend buffet – makes this a cheap and cheerful place to eat. If you don't fancy sitting in the no frills interior, then £3.50 gets you a takeaway box you can fill to the brim with anything you like. All in all, Dou Dou is a reasonable bet if you're after a cruelty-free meal.

£
Vegan

The Fields Beneath ❹

CAFÉ STAPLES

52a Prince of Wales Road, NW5 3LN
Tel: 020 7424 8838
www.thefieldsbeneath.com
Insta: @fieldsbeneath
Travel: Kentish Town West LO, Chalk Farm LU
Open: Mon-Fri 7am to 4pm, Sat 8am to 5pm, Sun 9am to 5pm

You can't ask for much more from a vegan café like The Fields Beneath: a warm, laid-back space; delicious wraps, burgers, sandwiches and sausage rolls, as well as sweet pastries, a bevvy of beverages and it's all completely cruelty free. Since making the decision to ditch dairy, their food has really come into its own, and the Fields Beneath now offers some of the best café staples to be found in London.

Their specials are worth scouting out too – we had spicy Mac'n'Cheese, and a Blood Orange Bakewell that was freshly baked and delicious. You don't have to break the bank here with salads for under a fiver, sandwiches and other substantial meals for just a quid or two more, and plenty of hot drinks and pastries for just two to three pounds. The café is located under the railway arches of Kentish Town West Station, one of a number of small but eclectic businesses that include the Camden Town Brewery (all their beers are vegan too!) and Lunar Cycles. You'll be hard pressed to miss it though, as they've left an array of comical road signs out to indicate what waits within their premises. One of London's best vegan eateries.

£
Vegan

Hawraman Café ❺
MEDITERRANEAN

38 Chalk Farm Road, NW1 8AJ
Tel: 020 7813 2908
www.hawramancamdencafe.com
Travel: Chalk Farm LU
Open: Sun-Thurs 10:30am-8:30pm, Fri-Sat 10:30am-9:30pm

This Camden café is a rustic eatery serving a selection of staple dishes from Mediterranean cuisine in a casual, yet cosily decorated interior. Here you can expect to find things like baba ganoush, falafel and halloumi salads, alongside a range of lighter dishes and drinks. Everything is vegetarian, but they also serve some vegan and gluten free options. The tables are spread out in a communal style, and the owners encourage sharing space with your neighbours, so don't count on an intimate escape here. What you can expect is that the food will be fresh, good quality and won't leave you feeling guilty or bloated afterwards. They also have outdoor seating at the back and front for when the weather is fine, plus a spot by the fireplace for when it's not. The prices are reasonable for Camden with mains costing between £5 and £10. It's a pleasant place to eat, and serves food that feels a lot more authentic than the usual fare in the area, which is largely dominated now by big chains.

£-££
Vegetarian
Some Vegan
Some Gluten Free

Magic Falafel ⑥

FALAFEL

Unit 708, Stables Market, 31 Chalk Farm Road,
Camden Town, NW1 8AH
Tel: 074 8264 6499
www.camdenmarket.com/food-drink/magic-falafel
Twitter: @Magic-falafel/Insta: @Magic_falafel
Travel: Camden Town LU
Open: Daily 10am-8pm

For years falafel has been the go-to vegetarian fast food, long before seitan chicken wings and tofish captured our imaginations. Many an establishment has claimed that theirs is the gold standard, but with a plethora of Middle Eastern and speciality eateries now all over London, it takes a lot to stand out from the crowd. And doing just that is Magic Falafel – a relative newcomer with a rapidly growing reputation for serving top quality fritters and pittas. They also do salad boxes jam packed with tasty fresh vegetables, with the fried aubergines worthy of special mention. With a couple of locations in Camden's Lock and Stables Markets, they're hard to miss amid the foodie furore, especially as they're a vegan and gluten free establishment. They're not cheap, with pittas and salad boxes between £7 and £10, but these guys would give most local kebab shops a run for their money.

Aside from the all important tahini and hummus, they also serve a good curry sauce or chilli to accompany your meal. If you're in town and up for a spot of al fresco dining, don't forget to bear Magic Falafel in mind, or if London's weather keeps you indoors then Deliveroo is at hand to help.

£
Vegetarian
Vegan
Some Gluten Free

Manna ➐
INTERNATIONAL FINE DINING

4 Erskine Road, NW3 3AJ
Tel: 020 7722 8028
www.mannav.com
Travel: Chalk Farm LU
Open: Tues-Fri 12noon-3pm & 6.30pm-10pm,
Sat 12noon-3pm & 6pm-10pm, Sun 12noon-8.30pm

A stone's throw from Primrose Hill is the oldest surviving vegetarian restaurant in London, which celebrated its 50th anniversary in 2017. Manna is now 100% vegan and looks entirely different from its origins in north London's 1960's counterculture. Today it offers a more fine dining experience than most other plant-based eateries in the capital. A curated selection of dishes from world cuisine is on the menu, with Jamaican stews featuring alongside mezzes – and the chef's daily special is nearly always one to look out for. Lots of raw and gluten free options are available too, in keeping with Manna's desire to promote healthy eating.

The space isn't bedecked with chandeliers, but the white tablecloth service during the evenings makes for a more upmarket vegan dinner date out than is otherwise readily available. Mains are fairly expensive in comparison to other London vegan eateries, at £15 a head, and for a full course meal you should expect to spend at least £30 per head. Manna's origins can be seen in the photos scattered about the restaurant showing the restaurant's early days. The place may have changed but there is a continuity here which we hope endures for many years to come.

£££
Vegan
Some Gluten Free and Raw

Mildred's Camden ❽
INTERNATIONAL
9 Jamestown Road, Camden Town, NW1 7BW
Tel: 020 7482 4200
www.mildreds.co.uk/camden
Full review see page 56

Nectar Café ❾
HEALTH FOOD CAFÉ
57 Jamestown Road, NW1 7DB
Tel: 020 7483 3344
www.nectarcafe.co.uk
Insta: @nectarcafetriyoga
Travel: Camden Town LU
Open: Daily 8am-8pm

Found inside the in-demand Triyoga studio in Camden, Nectar Café is a vegetarian diner with a clean eating approach. It serves 'health foods' to those in need of a pre or post-workout boost. Raw, vegan and gluten free options abound among the range of salad bowls, wraps and smoothies on offer. You'll also be able to enjoy hot drinks and snacks like protein balls or brownies. The seating area is communally orientated, with large tables and benches shared between customers, so don't anticipate tucking yourself away in a corner here. Prices are fairly steep; small smoothies will set you back nearly £5 and salads are around £8. Nectar Café is a little out of the way to warrant a visit in its own right, but serves its purpose as a healthy vegetarian café for the yoga crowd using the studio.

£
Vegetarian
Some Gluten Free and Raw
Some Vegan

Purezza ⑩
VEGAN PIZZA
43 Parkway, NW1 7PN
Tel: 020 3884 0078
www.purezza.co.uk
Twitter/Insta: @purezzauk
Travel: Camden Town LU
Open: Sun-Thurs 12noon-10pm, Fri-Sat 12noon-11pm

Not all good things come from London, and Purezza is here to prove it. Born in Brighton, they're the UK's first vegan pizzeria, and have enjoyed such success that they've got a second branch under their belt in one of the capital's biggest plant-based culinary hubs. With over 10 flavours of pizza on the menu, as well as pasta dishes, sides and desserts, Purezza offers a complete vegan take on the Italian dining experience. Expect infamous Italian indulgences like lasagne and tiramisu, classic toppings like margherita and marinara, as well as more great comfort foods like mac'n'cheese and dough balls. Their drinks menu is ample too, with both alcoholic and non-alcoholic drinks aplenty. Pizzas and mains range between £6 and £12, and sides and sweet things are reasonably priced, so you needn't break the bank for an evening meal here. There's plenty of space in the simply furnished restaurant, and you can see what's going on with that wood burning oven in the kitchen. Purezza are a great example of the transformation in London's vegan scene and judging from their busy Camden outpost, they are here to stay.

££
Vegan
Some Gluten Free and Raw

Rudy's Dirty Vegan Diner ⑪
AMERICAN DINER

Unit 739 Camden Stables Market, NW1 8AH
Twitter/Insta: @rudysDVD
Travel: Camden Town LU
Open: Daily 11am-7pm

Doing veganism the dirty way has become popular among many followers of the lifestyle, not least on account of the tired association with salads and bean stews. As you might be able to tell from their name, Rudy's is one such establishment, and they're doing their bit for those ditching meat, while unabashedly shouting it from the rafters.

A glance at their food shows they're doing it the right way. No longer do you have to forgo stacked up Reuben sandwiches, buffalo wings or 'dirty dogs', for all manner of meaty and messy things can be found here. The open kitchen allows you to see your food being prepared and there is plenty of seating in and around the Stables Market so you can relax and enjoy your vegan treat. It's a tad more expensive than competing junk food eateries, with burgers costing around £8, sides for around half of this and meal deals for £10. We're not complaining that Camden Market has another vegan eatery though, and the loyal crowd round here aren't either.

£-££
Vegan

Square Root Camden ⑫

SODA AND ICE CREAM

KERB, Unit 62, The Loft, Camden Lock Place, NW1 8AF
www.squarerootsoda.co.uk
Insta: @squarerootcamden
Travel: Camden Town LU
Open: Mon-Thurs 11am-6pm, Fri-Sat 11am-7pm

This Hackney-based institution has deservedly made a name for itself in recent years, with their handmade sodas having won the BBC's Best Drinks Producer award in 2015. Not only have many shops in London been scrambling to get some of their limited, small batch stuff, but Square Root have now also opened a soda bar in the heart of Camden's foodie scene.

The brand is known for producing all the classics like cola, lemonade and elderflower, but here you'll find a seasonally rotating menu of quirkier fruity fizzes, such as mango soda, citrus crush and non-alcoholic sbalgiato. Drinks can be accessorized with raspberries and other fruits, or turned into floats and sundaes with vegan ice creams, thick sauces and chunks of brownie. A cup of soda costs £2.50 or upgrade to a float or ice cream sundae for a couple of quid more. You'll be hard-pressed to find a drink more satisfying than a Square Root soda on a hot summer's day, but whatever the weather they've got it covered – hot chocolates and small sweet treats are always available.

£
Vegan
Gluten Free
Raw

Temple of Camden ⑬
VEGAN FRIED CHICKEN

103A Camley Street, N1C 4PF
www.templeofseitan.co.uk
Insta: @templeofseitan
Travel: King's Cross LU
Open: Mon-Sat 11am-9pm, Sun 11am-6pm

Sister store to the Seitan outpost in Hackney that is London's first vegan chicken shop, the Temple of Camden brings a slightly more dine-in vibe to the brand, with a coolly designed space and extra indoor seating. They also have more options, including 'hamburgers', pastries and hot drinks. This is one of the best ways to indulge in something that feels naughty, but isn't, and makes for some fairly Instagrammable grub too. Seitan – essentially a wheat cake – by and large has the taste, texture and appearance of chicken, and when wedged between a bun and with all the extras you really can't tell the difference. This is a little less the case with the wings, but these are still a tasty treat alongside a box of chips and a soft drink. At between £5 and £7 for burgers, wings and wraps (and considerably less for sides and sweet things), the Temple is price competitive with KFC, and is so much better on all fronts, showing that you don't need chicken to satisfy those Kentucky fried cravings. One of our favourite vegan food brands, Temple of Seitan's three outposts are perfect places to eat, whatever the weather.

Branches:
Temple of Hackney
10 Morning Lane, E9 6NA, see page 284

Temple Goods Café
Hackney Downs Studios, 17 Amhurst Terrace, E8 2BT, see page 138

£
Vegan
Some Gluten Free

VBurger ⑭

BURGERS

215-216, Camden Lock Market,
Chalk Farm Road, NW1 8AF
Tel: 079 5620 3256
www.vburger.co.uk
Insta: @vburgercamden
Travel: Camden Town LU
Open: Sun-Thu 11am-7pm, Fri-Sat 11am-9pm

Among a handful of meal-free eateries popping in and around the Camden Lock area, VBurger serves what you might expect from first hearing its name – 100% plant based patties in a bun with some more veg. There are few options to select from, and the drinks and sides menus are similarly limited, but as this is a stall that you visit when passing through the market, you're unlikely to have exhausted them all anytime soon. Falafel or mushroom burgers can be enjoyed with a Coke and onion rings for around £10, but if you want a beet or seitan burger individually, they cost £7. There is a small counter top facing the kitchen where you can sit down and eat, but don't expect an intimate occasion or sheltered seating of any kind when visiting. VBurger is an appetising vegan alternative to the local fast food joints in the area,

£
Vegan

What the Pitta! ⑮
VEGAN KEBAB
89-91 Bayham Street, NW1 0AG
www.whatthepitta.com
Twitter/Insta:@whatthepitta
Travel: Camden Town LU
Open: Sun-Weds 11.30am-9pm, Thurs-Sat 11.30am-11pm

A fitting name for a restaurant serving kebabs that'll make you exclaim just how meaty their döner dopplegängers taste, while managing to be 100% vegan. What the Pitta's success has seen them extend their roots beyond Box Park and they've now set up their third venture in town – a nu-age kebab shop in Camden. The menu is small, but has everything you really need – döner boxes, lahmacuns and mezze, as well as soft drinks, beers, and baklava for the sweet toothed. The chunks of spicy soya in What the Pitta's boxes are full of flavour, and with pitta, salad and chips are just as good, if not better, than the meaty alternative. Carnivores have no excuse, and anyone who thought this stuff was reserved for nights out with inhibited decision making can think again. Prices are competitive, with most meals costing £8 and none more than £12. The spaces themselves are much alike, with enough seating for those wanting to eat in and minimal décor. What the Pitta! is the perfect antidote to the capital's meaty street food.

Branches:

Box Park Croydon, Unit 9,
99 George Street, CR0 1LD, see p.231

Box Park Shoreditch, Unit 52,
2-10 Bethnal Green Road, E1 6GY, see p.309

£
Vegan

Young Vegans 16

PIE AND MASH

60 Camden Lock Place, NW1 8AF
www.youngvegans.co.uk
Twitter: @YoungvegansLDN/
Insta: @youngvegans
Travel: Camden Town LU
Open: Daily 11am-9pm

After a string of successful stalls at markets, events and festivals across the country, the team at Young Vegans have opened a permanent outlet at Camden Lock. They're a pie and mash shop with a reputation for serving top-notch cruelty-free comfort food, from a menu that rotates specials regularly enough so that you won't get bored of the same flavours. You can also look forward to their permanent menu of steak and ale, all-day breakfast, curry and sweet potato pies. All of these are served with a hearty dollop of creamy mash and gravy. For the sweet-toothed, there'll be something here for you too – think mud pies and fried brownies. All pies are £7, and you can top up with desserts and drinks for £10. The portions are plentiful and you'll leave feeling satisfied.

Seating is limited, with just a handful of stools and surfaces to eat from inside, and a school bench for dining al fresco. Their pies are also available via Deliveroo, or to order as a box of 6 for eating at home (and which can be delivered across the UK). Young Vegans continue to operate at music events and festivals across the country, as well as at the Hackney Downs Vegan Market on a regular basis, so there are plenty of opportunities to try this unique vegan take on meaty classics.

£
Vegan
Some Gluten Free

Hampstead

Rani
GUJARATI

7 Long Lane, N3 2PR
Tel: 020 8349 2636
www.rani.uk.com
Travel: Finchley Central LU
Open: Mon-Fri 11am-3pm & 6pm-11pm,
Sat-Sun 12noon-4.30pm & 6pm-11pm

Rani is a popular and long standing local Indian restaurant that has been serving the curry needs of Finchleyites for over 30 years. Specialising in vegetarian Gujarati cuisine, they've got plenty of dishes to try out, from your typical chickpea and aubergine fare to less commonly found spiced bananas in gravy. Of course, this can all be enjoyed alongside naans, daals and rice dishes in a pleasantly decorated interior that makes for a nice spot to relax and sample authentic Gujarati food. The buffets are particularly good value – prices vary between £8.95 and £15 per head (depending at what time of the day and week you go), but those with a hearty appetite will find their 'all you can eat' policy, great value. Perhaps not one to travel far for, but a sound option when in the area, Rani certainly knows how to make good curry.

££
Vegetarian

BRANCH

Woodlands Hampstead
SOUTH INDIAN

Hampstead, 102 Heath Street, NW3 1DR
www.woodlandsrestaurant.co.uk
Full review see page 51

Hendon

Rose Vegetarian
ASIAN

532-534 Kingsbury Road, NW9 9HH
Tel: 020 8905 0025
www.rosevegetarian.co.uk
Travel: Kingsbury LU
Open: Mon-Sun 12noon-10pm

This quirky spot is hard to define – Rose Vegetarian has for years been run by the same Bombay family, who mash up tandoori sizzlers side by side with Chinese noodle soups on their kitschy pink menus. If you're select about what you try - think aloo tikki or samosa chaats rather than chow meins – then this is actually a fantastic place to get a taste of non-Anglicised, authentic Indian food. The interior itself will be familiar to anyone who has visited casual diners on the Indian subcontinent, which perhaps contributes to the spot's popularity among the local Asian community. The portions are very generous and the prices kept low, with buffets costing just £6 and full meals around the same. Not one we expect you'll be travelling far for, but it's the best eatery in the area. Vegan options are available.

£
Vegetarian
Some Vegan

Engocha

Holloway, Crouch Hill & Tufnell Park

Restaurants, Cafés & Bars:

1) Cookies and Scream
2) Engocha
3) EZ and Moss
4) Healthy Wealthy
5) Jai Krishna
6) Loving Hut
7) Vegan Yes

Shops:

A) The Third Estate, p.346

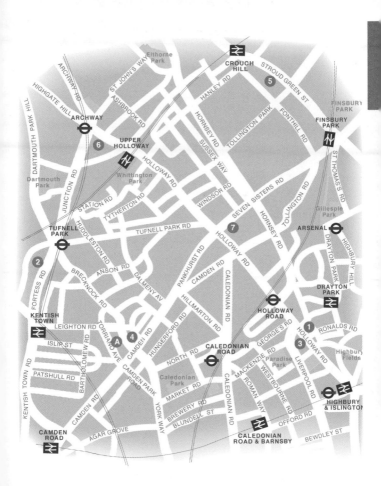

CROUCH HILL
STROUD GREEN ST
5
FINSBURY PARK
FINSBURY PARK
ELTHORNE PARK
ST JOHN'S WAY
ARCHWAY RD
ASHBROOK RD
HIGHGATE HILL
HANLEY RD
HORNSEY RD
TOLLINGTON PARK
FONTHILL RD
ARCHWAY
6
UPPER HOLLOWAY
SUSSEX WAY
HOLLOWAY RD
ST THOMAS'S RD
DARTMOUTH PARK HILL
Dartmouth Park
Whittington Park
JUNCTION RD
STATION RD
WINDSOR RD
SEVEN SISTERS RD
HORNSEY RD
TOLLINGTON RD
Gillespie Park
TYTHERTON RD
ARSENAL
DRAYTON PARK
HIGHBURY HILL
TUFNELL PARK
HUDDLESTON RD
TUFNELL PARK RD
7
HOLLOWAY RD
2
FORTESS RD
BRECKNOCK RD
ANSON RD
DALMENY AV
PANKHURST RD
CAMDEN RD
CALEDONIAN RD
DRAYTON PARK
HILLMARTON RD
HOLLOWAY ROAD
RONALDS RD
1
KENTISH TOWN
LEIGHTON RD
TORRIANO AVE
HUNGERFORD RD
NORTH RD
GEORGE'S RD
3
Highbury Fields
ISLIP ST
A
4
CAMDEN RD
CAMDEN PARK ROAD
CALEDONIAN ROAD
MACKENZIE RD
Paradise Park
LIVERPOOL RD
HOLLOWAY RD
PATSHULL RD
BARTHOLOMEW RD
Caledonian Park
ROMAN WAY
WESTBOURNE RD
HIGHBURY & ISLINGTON
KENTISH TOWN RD
CAMDEN RD
MARKET RD
CALEDONIAN RD
YORK WAY
BREWERY RD
BLUNDELL ST
OFFORD RD
CAMDEN ROAD
AGAR GROVE
CALEDONIAN ROAD & BARNSBY
BEWDLEY ST

Cookies and Scream ❶
VEGAN & GLUTEN FREE BAKERY & DESSERTS
130 Holloway Road, N7 8JE
www.cookiesandscream.com
Insta: @cookiesandscreambakery
Travel: Holloway Road LU
Open: Sun-Thurs 10am-8pm, Fri-Sat 10am-9pm

Following their great success at their now defunct venue in
Camden, Cookies and Scream opened on Holloway Road
and have continued to thrive. A vegan, gluten-free bakery and
desserts diner, they offer a bewildering choice of flavours of
dairy-free cakes, cookies and shakes. Health food is strictly
off the agenda– their delicious produce is sugar rich, and
unsuitable for anyone with nut or soya intolerances.

For a small outlet, Cookies and Scream have developed
quite a following, which has surely been helped by their
Instagram page showing off doughnuts slathered in thick
chocolate sauce, and Victoria sponges oozing with jam. Their
popularity translates into how fast the day's batches sell out
so get down early if you can. The interior is limited to a few
small tables and chairs to perch on, but there is outdoor
seating on sunny days. The prices are very reasonable –
expect to pay £2 for hot beverages, £4 for milkshakes and
between £3 and £5 for a generous dessert. If you're looking to
pig out then Cookies and Scream is really worth a visit for any
vegan, veggie or omnivore with a sweet tooth.

£
Vegan
Gluten Free

Engocha ❷

ETHIOPIAN

143 Fortess Road, NW5 2HR
Tel: 020 7485 3838
Travel: Tufnell Park LU
Open: Mon-Sat 11am-8pm, Sun 11am-7pm

Engocha is an Ethiopian diner that doles out quality grub, that also happens to be healthy, vegan and inexpensive. They serve traditional stews alongside rice or injera – a doughy flatbread native to the Horn of Africa –that can be enjoyed as a platter for 3, 4 or 5, for £5, £7 and £9 respectively. These curried stews bring together an abundance of leafy greens and legumes, with an intriguing mix of herbs and spices too. Everything is gluten & nut-free and vegan, and eating here is guaranteed to leave you feeling fresh and wholesome. Engocha take great pride in their Ethopian coffee which is hand roasted to order and is deliciously strong; it comes in the traditional way with smoking frankincense to add to the occasion. The dining space is a simple one, with just a few tables and chairs, and no toilet, so prepare yourself for a no-frills experience that is solely about the food.

£
Vegan
Gluten Free

EZ and Moss ❸
HOMEMADE CAFÉ STAPLES
183 Holloway Road, N7 8LX
Twitter: @EZandMoss
Travel: Holloway Road LU
Open: Mon-Fri 8am-5pm, Sat-Sun 9am-5pm

When looking to escape the bustle of N7's Holloway Road, EZ and Moss is a welcome world away from neighbouring seedy bookies and kebab shops. A tranquil indie café attracting a different crowd of locals to those filling the terraces on match day, here you'll find a range of great hot beverages and freshly made vegan and vegetarian foods. Sweet treats sit in harmony with healthier meals – enjoy a fluffy muffin and matcha latte, or follow a light salad or veggie breakfast with an AllPress coffee.

The menu changes often and features a daily rotation of specials, but salads, stews, burgers and brunch dishes are regulars, all full of flavour and colour. We're keenest on their fruity porridges and granolas. EZ and Moss is an inviting setting, with a minimal, white-walled interior, wooden surfaces and charming details like light bulb saltshakers. The service is friendly and personal too and you can see your food being prepared behind the counter as you wind down with a coffee. £5-£10 gets you brunch and a hot drink, so the pricing is fair and competitive with nearby options. Highly recommended.

£
Vegetarian
Some Gluten Free and Raw

Healthy Wealthy ❹
INDIAN THALIS AND SWEETS
10 Brecknock Road, N7 0DD
Tel: 020 7700 0777
www.healthywealthyvegan.co.uk
Insta: @HealthyWealthy
Travel: Caledonian Road LU
Open: Mon-Sat 11am-9pm

This little north London establishment is as good a spot as any for getting thali in the city, and it's all vegan and almost entirely gluten free. To the uninitiated, thalis are steel tray platters of curry that are great for getting a taste of everything, and are traditionally eaten with the hands, using rice and bread to mop up the vegetable and legume rich curries. The dishes at Healthy Wealthy are some of the most wholesome and tasty around, and if you look beyond the no-frills set up, you'll have found yourself a little gem. Expect saag and daal, samosas and pakoras aplenty, all of which can be enjoyed inexpensively. You can tuck into a thali for as little as £5 with extras for around £1. There is also a selection of Indian sweets and cakes available for around £2 each. This is a solid local option when seeking out good Indian fare and is just opposite Third Estate for all your vegan, ethical clothing and footwear needs (see p. 346)

£
Vegan
Mostly Gluten Free

Jai Krishna ⑤
INDIAN VEGETARIAN
161 Stroud Green Rd, N4 3PZ
Tel: 020 7272 1680
Travel: Crouch Hill LO/ Manor House LU
Open: Monday-Saturday 12noon-2pm & 5.30pm-11pm

Stroud Green residents are lucky to have such a popular local Indian restaurant on their doorstep, and one which is also among the cheapest in this book – curries start from as little as £3.50. The menu is diverse and takes inspiration from across the Indian subcontinent. Some of our favourites are heavier daals from the North, and mango and buttermilk curries, called kalan, from the South. These are of course best enjoyed alongside a range of side dishes and snacks that are as inexpensive as the mains. For a comprehensive meal expect to pay around £8.

The space is intriguing – colourful renditions of Krishna and Christ stand side by side against red walls, giving a taste of India's colourful diversity. There's no meat on the menu but vegans should double check if ghee and paneer feature in their preferred dish. The only down side we can find about this cheap and cheerful eatery is that it's a bit out of the way, but you'll still need to book at weekends. Despite the trek, it's worth making your way to N4 with your own bottle of booze to see what Jai Krishna's is all about.

£
Vegetarian

Loving Hut ⑥
CHINESE & VIETNAMESE
669 Holloway Road, N19 5SE
Tel: 020 7281 8989
www.archway.lovinghut.co.uk
Travel: Archway LU
Open: Tue-Fri 12noon-3pm & 6pm-11pm,
Sat-Sun 6pm-11pm

Part of the flourishing vegan scene on Holloway Road, Loving Hut is a worldwide chain, with an Asian-centric menu largely fleshed out by faux meat dishes. It's popular with locals and visiting vegans alike, drawn by a cuisine that traditionally has been inseparable from animal products. This heritage has evidently inspired the menu too – think faux prawn, faux chicken, faux duck – all of which has been fried and battered, and is usually served with glutinous noodles or pancakes and salty sauces.

Slabs of sickly sweet cheesecake or banana fritters are our favourite way to wrap up a meal here. The food is tasty, but heavily processed, making for not entirely guilt-free dining. Prices are between £5-£10 for a meal, making it good value compared with many London alternatives. The interior is charmingly kitsch too, giving the place a down-to-earth vibe. Loving Hut is everything you'd want and expect from a cheap, canteen-style eatery.

£
Vegan

BRANCH

Vegan Yes ⑦
ITALIAN KOREAN FUSION
22 Seven Sisters Road, Nag's Head Market, N7 6AG
Tel: 079 3302 8570
www.veganyes.uk
Full review see page 305

Kensal Rise

Paradise Unbakery

INTERNATIONAL HEALTH FOODS
59 Chamberlayne Road, NW10 3ND
Tel: 020 8968 8321
www.paradiseunbakery.com
Twitter: @paradiseunbaker/Insta: @paradiseunbakery
Travel: Kensal Rise LO/Kensal Green LU
Open: Weds-Mon 9am-5pm

After a successful few seasons running from market stalls across the country, Paradise Unbakery has opened a permanent shop in Kensal Rise. Here they serve homemade vegan breakfasts, lunches, coffees and cake. It's largely a raw, sugar and gluten-free eatery too, so you needn't feel guilty when indulging here. There are plenty of diverse dishes on offer here, such as breakfast bagels and smoothie bowls, pancakes or porridge, and tasty main meals during lunch service including a posh mac 'no' cheese, moussaka and raw lasagne. The price of breakfasts and mains ranges from £4.50 to £9.50, with plenty in between, making Paradise Unbakery competitively priced. They've also got a small but growing grocery and to-go section. There are plenty of tables and chairs however if you do want to sit in, and the space is pleasantly decorated with houseplants and matching wallpaper. Whether looking for a spiced latte, fruity smoothie or a raw meal, Paradise Unbakery hits the spot.

£
Vegan
Some Raw
Some Gluten Free and Raw

Comptoir V

MOROCCAN FUSION

Keslake Mansions, Station Terrace, NW10 5RU
Tel: 020 3092 0047
www.comptoirv.co.uk
Twitter / Insta: @comptoirvlondon / comptoir_v
Travel: Kensal Rise LO
Open: Daily 12noon-10pm

This vegan restaurant is a gem for locals, and well worth making a trip to north London for. The menu is largely a Moroccan & Caribbean fusion, but includes highlights from cuisines around the world, in a mash-up that makes for some fab and original food. Their mac and cheese and mushroom ribs' is a firm favourite, but aunty Esi curry (a Ghanaian dish) and banana and date crumble are equally appetising. They offer big plates, small plates and a range of sides like plantain and ghife bread, so Comptoir V is ideal for group dining. Nearly everything is packed with colourful veg and avoids gluten, so you won't feel guilty no matter how much you indulge. Cool craft beers and other drinks are aplenty, meaning you can make a night of it here. The space is stylishly decorated in a Moroccan manner, equipped with souk styled brass lamps, tables and blue ceramic plates. With plentiful portions, £5 for small plates and £10 for big plates translates to great value, and there are lots of sides and drinks for less. Comptoir V deserves to be better known and is well worth a special trip to Kensal Rise.

££
Vegan
Some Gluten Free

Skip Garden Kitchen

King's Cross, Euston & Islington

Restaurants, Cafés & Bars:

Drummond Street
    1) Chutney's
    2) Diwana Bhel Poori House
    3) Ravi Shankar
4) Indian Veg Bhelpoori House
5) Itadaki Zen
6) Jaz and Jul's Chocolate House
7) Mildred's King's Cross
8) Skip Garden Kitchen
9) VX London

CANAL REACH ⑧
HANDYSIDE ST
CAMLEY ST
COPENHAGEN ST
CALEDONIAN RD
RICHMOND AVE
Barnard Park
Granary Building
Granary Square
St Pancras Gardens
Camley St Nature Reserve
YORK WAY
Regent's Canal
CARNEGIE ST
BARNSBURY RD
PURCHESE ST
MIDLAND RD
PANCRAS RD
GOODS WAY
KING'S BLVD
WHARFDALE RD ⑨
CALEDONIAN RD
WYNFORD RD
RODNEY ST
CALSHOT ST
KILLICK ST
COLLIER ST
CHAPEL ST ⑥
④
ST PANCRAS STATION
KINGS CROSS STATION
Joseph Grimaldi Park
⑦
ISLINGTON
OSSULSTON ST
British Library
Midland Hotel
EUSTON RD
PENTONVILLE RD
KING'S CROSS RD
⑤

EVERSHOLT ST
EUSTON STATION
HAMPSTEAD RD
STARCROSS ST
DRUMMOND ST
EUSTON ST
N GOWER ST
MELTON ST
Euston Square Gardens
EUSTON RD
GOWER PL
① ③② ③

Drummond Street
SOUTH INDIAN

Chutney's ❶
124 Drummond Street, NW1 2PA; Tel: 020 7388 0604
www.chutneyseuston.uk; Travel: Euston Square LU;
Open: Daily 12noon-11pm

Diwana Bhel Poori House ❷
121-123 Drummond Street, NW1 2PA; Tel: 020 7387 5556
www.diwanabph.com; Travel: Euston Square LU;
Open: Mon-Sat 12noon-11:30pm, Sun 12noon-10:30pm

Ravi Shankar Bhel Poori ❸
133-135 Drummond Street, NW1 2HL; Tel: 020 7388 6458
www.ravishankarbhelpoori.com; Travel: Euston Square;
Open: Daily 12noon-11pm

Drummond Street is known for its concentration of Indian and
Bangladeshi restaurants, all offering great value, delicious food.
Three in particular stand out. Diwana Bhel Poori House claims
to be the oldest vegetarian South Indian restaurant in London.
Here you'll find thalis, dosas and curries aplenty. Chutney's
and Ravi Shankar offer similar fare but also have a buffet
during lunch times and à la carte in the evenings. Of the three,
Diwana has a more extensive menu, but all have vegan options.
Vegans should always ask if their dish contains ghee or paneer
(butter and curd cheese), which are both found extensively in
this cuisine. Tasty meals cost between £5 and £10, making
Drummond Street a great place for no-fuss veggie Indian food.
Remember to bring your own bottle.

£
Vegetarian
Some Vegan

Indian Veg Bhelpoori House ❹
INDIAN BUFFET
92-93 Chapel Market, N1 9EX
Tel: 020 7837 4607
www.theindianveg.wordpress.com
Travel: Angel LU
Open: Daily 12noon-11.30pm

After years of dishing out great value veggie fare, this north London institution has acquired a loyal following and is always popular with local workers looking for a cheap and tasty lunch. Bhelpoori House offers a simple setting within which to enjoy a freshly prepared array of hearty curries and sides – all self-service as an all-you-can-eat buffet.

You can be sure that all the dishes are vegetarian and they've got vegan options too. It's also great value with £7.95 entitling you to graze until your heart's content and takeaway options cost even less. Humorous posters of vegetarian propaganda line the walls, providing information and jokes on this diet and lifestyle. They claim to be an eco-friendly establishment as well as abstaining from animal products and provide free takeaway food to homeless people in the area. It might feel a little dated in here, and you need to bring your own booze, but it remains one of the best places in Islington if you're looking to eat meat free.

£
Vegetarian
Some Vegan

Itadaki Zen ⑤
JAPANESE
139 King's Cross Road, WC1X 9BJ
Tel: 020 7278 3573
www.itadakizen-uk.com
Travel: King's Cross LU
Open: Mon-Fri 12noon-3pm & 6pm-10pm, Sat 6pm-10pm

Japanese and vegan aren't usually two words used in the same sentence, but you can think again with Itadaki Zen. A short walk from King's Cross station and in an area with more vegan eateries than you can wave a stick at, this authentic and unique restaurant stands out from the crowd by offering a cruelty-free alternative to a cuisine that rarely excludes fish or meat of some kind. They've got an exceptionally well-curated array of set menus and sushi dishes to choose from, all of which incorporate essential Japanese ingredients and flavours and all of which are presented in the traditional Japanese style we've grown to love. You can choose from classics like miso and udon noodle soups, seaweed and spring vegetable sushi pieces and spring rolls. Our favourite is the Kansei-han Tanno set – not just for how well it's presented, but also because it's so jam-packed with flavour and good ingredients. The aesthetic appeal of the interior matches that of the food - the warm lighting, clay walls and wooden furnishing transports you straight to the orient. Seating is limited, despite the extra space in the back, so booking for the evening is recommended. Be prepared to spend £20 or more per person for a complete meal – everything is vegan, organic and prepared to order, so it's worth every penny. In short – come for an unusual vegan take on Japanese cuisine, make sure you book a table and enjoy an evening of culinary adventure in this cosy restaurant.

£££
Vegan
Some Gluten Free and Raw

Jaz and Jul's Chocolate House ❻
CAFÉ AND CHOCOLATIER
1 Chapel Market, N1 9EZ
Tel: 020 3583 4375
www.jazandjuls.co.uk
Travel: Angel LU
Open: Tues-Sun 10am-6pm

A short walk down the energetic course of Chapel Market is a chocoholic's heaven – Jaz and Jul's chocolate shop. A café cum hot chocolate specialist, they source and sell single origin powders and bars, and have begun serving sweet and savoury foods too. Many of these have chocolate infused into them including the black bean chilli or avocado on toast. It's intriguing to see how chocolate can be used in so many dishes, but the hot chocolate is a safe and delicious option. The fondues are a lot of fun too, and can be enjoyed with a glass of prosecco. There's plenty of seating and a friendly welcome here, making it a good place to enjoy a drink while whiling away an afternoon. The food prices range from £4.50-£9, fondues start at £12 and hot chocolates, both in-house or packaged to take home, are around the £3 mark. This is inexpensive when compared to quite a few of the capital's other chocolate specialists. We recommend Jaz and Jul's as a quirky spot to enjoy something we all love.

£-££
Vegetarian

BRANCH

Mildred's King's Cross ❼
INTERNATIONAL
200 Pentonville Road, N1 9JP
www.mildreds.co.uk
Full review see page 56

Jaz and Jul's Chocolate House

Skip Garden Kitchen ❽

COMMUNITY GARDEN AND KITCHEN

1 Tapper Walk, N1C 4AQ

Tel: 075 0692 1084

www.globalgeneration.org.uk

Twitter: @global_gen/

Insta: @globalgeneration

Travel: King's Cross LU/Camden Road LO

Open: Tues-Sat 10am-4pm

It's fantastic to still see grass roots food movements sprouting up amid the urban sprawl of central London, and Skip Garden embodies this perfectly. A patch of vibrancy that moves around the free space not used by building developments in King's Cross, here you'll find a site filled with fruit and veg grown in disused skips. The produce is put to good use in homely vegetarian and vegan meals cooked up and served from table tops in an outdoor seating space. Not only should Skip Garden be lauded for their organic gardening practices and community activism, but the food is fantastic too. Expect to find dishes ranging from quiche to curry, or tabbouleh to afternoon tea, all of which are light and flavoursome. To cover the costs involved with providing a service like this, they have a reasonable set price of £15 for a main and two sides per head which is great value. If you don't fancy al fresco dining then they have a quirky indoor space available too. The personal approach of Skip Garden means that they can cater for most needs; keep an eye on their website for regular pop-up dining events.

££

Vegetarian

Some Gluten Free, Vegan and Raw

VX London ❾
JUNKFOOD RESTAURANT AND SHOP
73 Caledonian Road, N1 9BT
Tel: 020 7833 2315
www.vx-london.com
Insta: @vxlondon
Travel: King's Cross LU
Open: Daily 10am-6.30pm

You might be surprised to find, situated on the least inspiring part of Caledonian Road, a vegan place of pilgrimage. Designed to be a 'one-stop shop' for all a vegan's needs, with cruelty-free junk food and graphic clothing from the Secret Society of Vegans brand. A peak at their Instagram reveals rainbow coloured cakes, thickly glazed doughnuts and faux chicken nuggets, all of which can be bought to takeaway or can be eaten in, albeit within a limited space.

VX's food is a good antidote to the tired message that 'veganism is boring' or that 'vegans only eat salad'– here all the foods are forbidden pleasures. The catch is that the product is all processed carb & sugar heavy and definitely more microwave than Michelin. These indulgent treats don't come at much of a cost with very few dishes costing more than £5. The prices are kept low because the place is clearly run by vegans on a mission to keep plant-free eating tasty and fun.

The shop side of things is more limited, but there are some fun novelty goods including mugs and tees proclaiming the vegan message. They are almost as much fun as the vegan junk food and make VX London a place well worth seeking out.

£
Vegan

Stoke Newington

Restaurants, Cafés & Bars:

1) Bodega 50
2) Haunt
3) Made in Hackney
   & Food for All
4) Rasa
5) Temple Goods

Shops:

STOKE
NEWINGTON

CAZENOVE RD

ABNEY PARK
CEMETERY

NORTHWOLD RD

STOKE
NEWINGTON
COMMON

YOAKLEY RD

STOKE NEWINGTON CHURCH ST

KERSLEY RD

D'NEVOR RD

LAWRENCE RD

RECTORY RD

DEFOE RD

OLDFIELD RD

KYNASTON RD

BROOKE RD

ALBION RD

DYNEVOR RD

VICTORIAN GROVE

STOKE NEWINGTON HIGH ST

LESWIN RD

BAYSTON RD

RECTORY
ROAD

BARBAULD RD

NEVILL RD

EVERING RD

MANSE RD

BEATTY RD

AMHURST RD

SYDNER RD

RECTORY RD

DOWNS RD

ALBION RD

MILTON GROVE

ALLEN RD

WALFORD RD

FOULDEN RD

HACKN
DOWN

BRIGHTON RD

STOKE NEWINGTON HIGH ST

FARLEIGH RD

AMHURST RD

PALANTINE RD

PRINCE GEORGE RD

SHACKLEWELL RD

Bodega 50 ❶
HOMEMADE CAFÉ STAPLES
50 Allen Road, N16 8RZ
Tel: 020 7683 3869
Insta: @bodega50
Travel: Rectory Road LO
Open: Daily 8am-6pm

Bodega – the Spanish word used for local grocery stores in New York – is a fitting name for this neighbourhood café that satisfies the vegan dining needs of the Stoke Newington crowd. Tucked away from the main road, Bodega 50 remains a little known gem that is treasured by its local patrons who come to enjoy the comforting food, coffee and relaxed atmosphere.

Simple lunch dishes like sourdough toasties, salads and soups are made fresh and priced low, which keeps it all just as sweet as the great pastries on offer. You won't be disappointed by their oat milk lattes either – they do full justice to the artisan coffee beans. In fact, the only things that aren't vegan are croissants and the occasional pastry, but just ask before you buy if you have any doubts.

The space inside has a cool Scandi vibe, is a good place to eat with kids and has an in-café dog called Bruce who is very amicable. You can enjoy a light breakfast or lunch and drink here for as little as £5. Bodega 50 might be hard to find but it is definitely one to seek out when visiting Stokey.

Branch:
442 Hoe Street, E17 9AH, see page 311

£
Vegan

Haunt ❷

AMERICAN DINER

182 Stoke Newington Road, N16 7UY

Tel: 020 7249 1203

www.hauntlondon.com

Insta: @hauntlondon

Travel: Stoke Newington/ Rectory Road LO

Open: Tue-Thur 5pm-11pm, Fri 5pm-2am,

Sat 12noon-2am, Sun 12noon-9pm

Haunt is one of our favourite vegan eating and events spaces in this trendy London hub. It started with a kitchen residency programme before setting up permanently with Biffs Jack Shack, serving brunches and jackfruit junk food, as well as an impressive range of craft beers, wines and cocktails. Burgers and wings are the main attractions, made from the miraculously meaty fruit that has become all the rage in the last few years, all perfectly paired with tasty toppings and sauces. The 'Samuel Hell Jackson' features hot sauce and jalapenos, while the 'New Jack City' plays on a classic using seitan pastrami and 'Gouda cheeze'. It's not only the names of dishes that are playful – here they experiment with all the extras a foodie could want, from blue cheese dips and maple butters to bourbon BBQ sauces. The space has an industrial chic feel to it, with bare brick walls contrasted by hanging plants, polished wooden tables and minimalist lighting. Haunt is dog friendly, and hosts regular events, from music performances to creative classes, making this a top place to come and hang out with friends. Unlike the great food, the prices are average, and for brunch or dinner you'll likely spend just over £10, or around £5 for a sizeable snack. Haunt is a great addition to the vegan scene – if you give them a try we're sure you'll be back for more.

£-££

Vegan

Some Gluten Free

Made in Hackney & Food for All ❸

3 Cazenove Road, N16 6PA
Tel: 020 8442 4266 & 020 8806 4138
www.madeinhackney.org & www.foodforall.co.uk
Travel: Stoke Newington LO
Made in Hackney open for consultation/classes only
Food For All open Mon-Fri 9am-6pm,
Sat 10am-6pm, Sun 11am-4pm

Made in Hackney is the kind of community initiative every borough needs. It's a kitchen and cookery school that runs regular courses and classes on how to live better, sharing personal, hands-on experiences of healthy vegan eating with thousands of people every year. One of the team's ambassador is Dr Rupy Aujla, who is soon to teach the UK's first culinary medicine course at Bristol University. The team also boasts professional chefs, activists and community engagers. Classes range from growing food in urban environments to cooking vegan junk food, while courses aim to teach skills that will establish a lifetime of plant-based cooking. Much of this is free or on a pay-by-donation basis. Made in Hackney also works with schools, charities and housing associations.

If you need the ingredients to start a plant-based diet Food For All is based at the entrance and is a health food shop that's been providing Hackney residents with vegetarian and vegan health products for over 40 years. Here you'll find locally made shea butters, herbal remedies, alongside affordable, high quality wholefoods. They too have many links to humanitarian causes, particularly with AMURT, a charity that focuses on community development and disaster relief. Made in Hackney and Food For All are ethical, independent and not-for-profit organisations that deserve your support.

Rasa

KERALAN

55 Stoke Newington Church Street, N16 0AR
Tel: 020 7249 0344
www.rasarestaurants.com
Travel: Stoke Newington LO
Open: Mon-Thurs 6pm-10.45pm, Fri 6pm-11:30pm, Sat 12noon-3pm & 6pm-11.30pm, Sun 12noon-3pm & 6pm-10.45pm

Think pink when you think Rasa – this Keralan restaurant stands out not only for its curries, but also for the eye-catching hue of its façade. This long-standing Stoke Newington institution has gained a reputation for serving unique and fresh vegetarian curries. The mixed curry platters served on a steel tray are a good way to sample a range of flavours from this style of South Indian cuisine, and specials like mango curries are worth a try.

You really can find all the colours of the rainbow in Rasa's food, with beets and bananas just a couple to mention from the extensive list of tropical fruits, vegetables and spices at play in the dishes. As always, rice and bread accompany these curries perfectly, the coconut rice being a real winner. Their sweet snacks and desserts are also intriguing and unusual so don't hold back from experimenting. There's plenty of vegan fare too and the dishes not containing ghee or paneer are clearly labelled. Curries cost £5.50 and you can pile up your plate with sides and rice or bread for a little extra. You'll likely total at around £10 for a good meal. It's always worth trying to book in advance, as Rasa are popular, but it repays the effort as this is one of north London's best veggie Indian restaurants.

£-££
Vegetarian

Temple Goods ❺
INTERNATIONAL
Hackney Downs Studios, 17 Amhurst Terrace, E8 2BT
www.templeofseitan.co.uk
Insta: @templegoodsuk
Travel: Rectory Road LO
Open: Mon-Fri 8am-4pm, Sat 10am-5pm, Sun 10am-3pm

As if the team behind the Temple of Seitan chain hadn't shaken up London's vegan scene enough with their hugely popular fried chicken shops, now they've brought the lucky residents of Hackney a quite different project. Temple Goods channels the brand's faux-meat loving ethos into a fully plant-based café. Tarts, toasties, fajitas and fry-ups are testament to how ditching meat is far from limiting. Fancy a Reuben but remembering you're banned from salami? Think again – these wizards with seitan have got it covered. And we're all left scratching our heads as to how they've made the vegan fried eggs have such a runny yolk. Boozy BBQ's are lined up most Thursday and Friday evenings too, meaning Temple Goods is a great place to eat and mingle with like-minded people. Prices are similar to their other spots, with meals costing between £5 and £8, and snacks and drinks between £2 and £4. There's plenty of indoor and outdoor seating, though this grub is perfect for when on the go. All veggies and vegans ought to visit, particularly when combined with a visit to Hackney Downs Vegan Market (see p.356) which takes place just outside every Saturday.

Branches:
Temple of Camden	Temple of Hackney
103a Camley Street, N1C 4PF	10 Morning Lane, E9 6NA
see page 89	see page 284

£
Vegan

Wood Green

Karamel Restaurant
INTERNATIONAL VEGAN FOOD AND LIVE MUSIC SPACE
4 Coburg Road, N22 6UJ
Tel: 020 8829 8989
www.karamelrestaurant.com
Travel: Alexandra Palace Rail/Turnpike Lane LU
Open: Mon-Fri 8am-11pm, Sat-Sun 10am-11pm

A local favourite with a more grown-up crowd, Karamel is a cultural events space for musicians, dramatists and comedians that doubles as a vegan diner, serving up hearty portions of pub-lunch grub and some extras borrowed from global cuisine. Bangers and mash sit alongside samosas and pizza, with gluten-free options available. The menu tends to change by the day, but it's all easy on the palate and varied enough that there's something for everyone here. Sunday roasts are the most expensive dish they serve but there's plenty at considerably cheaper price points, and you can reasonably expect to eat here for under £10. Despite the changing art on the walls, the interior is a little dull by day, but when the lights are dimmed for the evening service, the place gets a new lease of life. Karamel is a really good spot for anyone wanting to enjoy live performances in a friendly environment. They also serve alcohol including local beers on tap and are dog friendly. Take a look at their website to find out about future events, so you can combine great vegan food with live music.

£
Vegan
Some Gluten Free

...alternative Italian Pizza..

WEST

PickyWops

Clapham

Plantbase Café
CAFÉ STAPLES
2 Brighton Buildings, St John's Hill, SW11 1RZ
Tel: 020 7738 0555
Travel: Clapham Junction Rail
Open: Mon-Thurs 7am-8pm, Fri 7am-4pm, Sun 9am-8pm
You'll find Plantbase Café under the arches as you come out of Clapham Junction station. It's a small vegan eatery serving coffee and cake, as well as a couple of warm savoury options, such as a full English breakfast or curry, that are available to eat in or takeaway. The space is very limited, with just two or three tables, so don't come with expectations of silver service. The food is priced a little over the average rate, with hot meals costing between £7 and £10, and coffees and pastries for around £3 each. This is a solid vegan option when in need of food on the go in the Clapham area.

£
Vegan
Some Gluten Free and Raw

Fulham

222 Vegan Cuisine
INTERNATIONAL

222 North End Road, W14 9NU
Tel: 020 7381 2322
www.222vegancuisine.com
Twitter: @222VeganCuisine
Insta: @222vegancuisine
Travel: West Kensington LU
Open: Daily 12.30pm-3.30pm & 5.30pm-10.30pm

222 Vegan Cuisine is a popular eatery that's been serving strictly vegan food since 2004 in an unassuming manner and setting that makes for a good casual lunch out or more formal dinner. The cuisines on offer are diverse, with risottos and roasts as commonplace as stroganoffs and salads. The food is healthy and hearty, with organic produce used where possible.

Their buffets are worth particular mention – at £11.50 to eat in and £9.50 to take out, they really are all-you-can-eat and have a wide range of dishes, like quinoa salads and chickpea curries. Head chef, Ben Asamani, has established quite a reputation and for an evening meal it's advisable to book in advance. With careful lighting, a subtle soundtrack and attentive service, the effort will be rewarded with one of the best vegan fine dining experiences to be found in the capital.

££-£££
Vegan
Some Gluten Free and Raw

PickyWops
PIZZA

7 Shopping Palace, North End Road, SW6 1NN
Tel: 074 2707 6525
www.pickywops.com
Twitter/Insta: @pickywops
Travel: Fulham Broadway LU
Open: Mon-Thurs 6pm-11pm, Fri-Sun 12noon-11pm

This professional pizza chef duo really know their craft, and by combining it with veganism have brought something pretty special to town. PickyWops now have two branches, both of which are BYOB establishments – perfect for enjoying a bottle or two of beer as you munch into some quality, cruelty-free pizza. They offer an impressive range of 'cheeses' and bases from which to choose, including flavours like smoky coconut mozzarella and cashew nut Camembert as well as spirulina and hemp dough. There are a tonne of toppings to choose from too, which are as diverse as seitan salami and porcini to truffles and brocollini. They have some desserts and drinks of their own too, like Italian coffees and matcha twixx bites from a sisterly Italian food supplier, Pomodoro E Basilico. Prices range from £9 to £20 for pizza and calzone, depending on the toppings you choose, but you can get 7 inch pizzas and garlic bread for half this price, as well as desserts and drinks for between £2 and £4. With delivery and takeout service available, why choose anywhere else?

Branch:
95A Rye Lane, SE15 4ST, see p.226

££
Vegan

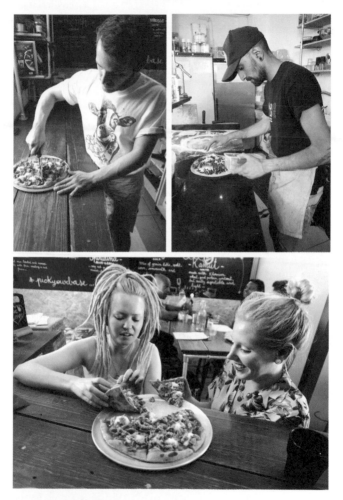

Hammersmith

The Gate
INTERNATIONAL FINE DINING
51 Queen Caroline Street, W6 9QL
Tel: 020 8748 6932
www.thegaterestaurants.com
Twitter: @GateRestaurant
Insta: @gaterestaurant
Travel: Hammersmith LU
Open: Mon-Fri 12noon-2.30pm & 6pm-10.30pm,
Sat 12noon-3pm & 5pm-10.30pm, Sun 12noon-9.30pm

With a reputation spanning 30 years, The Gate has earned itself
the right, alongside restaurant chains like Mildred's, to call itself
a vegetarian institution. Its aim is to offer a gourmet meat-free
dining experience across its three branches, by way of attractively
presented global cuisine served within their fashionably designed

spaces. The international menu features diverse dishes, but though you might find the odd curry or schnitzel, French and Italian food predominate. In particular we're big fans of the Tofu Tikka and Rotolo. The flavours are adventurous, showing that vegetarian (and vegan) food can be bold, and the presentation is artful without scrimping on portions. They also serve a host of great beers, wines and especially cocktails, giving a grown up appeal to the experience here.

The three branches can be characterised as 'modern chic', with high ceilings, sleek furniture and carefully designed lighting. The mains cost on average £15, with separate courses, sides and drinks for less, so a three course meal will likely cap at £40 per person. As happens with chains, you don't get the same sense of the individuality within each branch as you might with an independent, but The Gate still offers a rarely paralleled quality of food and service for vegans and vegetarians in London.

Branches:
The Gate Marylebone, 22-24 Seymour Place, W1H 7NL, see page 50
The Gate Islington, 370 St John St, EC1V 4N, see page 33

£££

Vegetarian
Vegan

Branch

Sagar
SOUTH INDIAN
157 King Street, W6 9JT
Tel: 020 8741 8563
www.sagarveg.co.uk
For review, see page 40

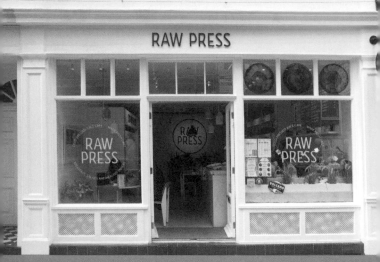

Kensington & Chelsea

Restaurants, Cafés & Bars:
1) Juicebaby
2) Raw Press
3) Tanya's Café
4) Wulf and Lamb

Shops:
A) Stella McCartney, p.335

Juicebaby ❶
VEGAN, GLUTENFREE AND RAW CAFÉ
398 King's Road, SW10 0LJ
www.juicebaby.co.uk
For review, see page 162

Raw Press ❷

VEGAN, GLUTEN-FREE AND RAW CAFÉ

3 Ellis Street, SW1X 9AL
Tel: 020 7730 4347
www.rawpress.co
Twitter/Insta: @rawpressco
Travel: Sloane Square LU
Open: Mon-Fri 8am-6pm, Sat 9am-6pm, Sun 9am-5pm

Raw Press have been at the forefront of the UK's raw food movement and specialise in cold-pressed juices. They proselytise this food preparation technique for both its health benefits and improved flavours and have a following of subscribers to their juice cleanse care packages. These are a great way to get closer to your 5-a-day but, visiting the café the food is very much to the fore.

Serving sweet and savoury dishes, salads and a couple of hot dishes throughout the day, the food here is colourful, healthy and freshly prepared. A must-try is the Instagram-worthy blueberries and buckwheat waffle, not least because it feels like an indulgence without really having any naughty ingredients to worry about. Free Wi-Fi and an inviting interior make this a great spot to convert into your impromptu office for an hour or two, but it's also a good place for a healthy break while shopping in the West Eend. Raw Press also offers a fantastic buffet service which is healthy and satisfying, but comes at fairly high price considering this is more café than restaurant. For those committed to a raw, vegan and gluten free diet, this is a great central London café and one well worth trying. Once you've tried their chia bowl with a green juice, chances are you'll be back for more.

££
Vegan
Gluten Free
Raw

Tanya's Café ❸
VEGAN, GLUTEN-FREE AND RAW CAFÉ
35 Ixworth Place, SW3 3QX
www.tanyasliving.com
Twitter: @TanyasLiving
Insta; @tanyasliving
Travel: South Kensington LU, Sloane Square LU
Open: Daily 7am-11pm

Tanya Mayer has become an online celebrity through her work as a raw vegan guru, promoting 'wellness' through a vegan and raw diet. Her success has allowed her to open a café in Chelsea and Kensington, the home of this trend, within the glamorously decorated indoor and outdoor space of MyChelsea boutique. The menu is supposed to support detoxing, and includes a selection of dishes inspired by classic recipes like lasagne and Pad Thai. The difference is that they are more like salads as they are almost entirely made up of raw vegetables. Expect to see the words 'probiotic' and 'activated' aplenty on the menu.

Tanya's also boasts a variety of cold-pressed juices, 'mylks' and spiced lattes – all of which are claimed to have medicinal properties. The food is carefully prepared but the prices are definitely on the high side with mains, which are essentially all salads, costing between £10 and £14. Tanya's is a great café serving tasty and interesting hot drinks and pastries, and is a sound option for an evening meal if you're in the Chelsea area.

££
Vegan
Gluten Free
Raw

Wulf and Lamb ④

INTERNATIONAL

243 Pavilion Road, SW1X 0BP
Tel: 020 3948 5999
www.wulfandlamb.com
Twitter/Insta: @wulfandlamb
Travel: Sloane Square LU
Open: Mon-Fri 7.30am-10pm
Sat 8am-10pm, Sun 9am to 9pm

Wulf and Lamb offers a chic vegan dining experience, as befits its salubrious Chelsea location. Found among a hub of shops and eateries on Pavilion Road, it serves global cuisine in a smartly designed but comfortable interior with outside seating at the front and a wonderful lush dining area to the rear which is perfect on fine days. Burgers, curry, chilli and pie can all be enjoyed here, or you can just opt for their delicious range of coffee and cakes.

Wulf and Lamb use locally sourced and organic produce wherever possible, some of which comes from Natoora down the road. They are more expensive than a lot of vegan eateries, with burgers and most other mains costing in the vicinity of £15, and sides and snacks costing between £4 and £6. They make up for the cost with plentiful portions, which have made this a popular eatery with locals and passing tourists. The food won't leave you feeling guilty, but perhaps the bill will, so Wulf and Lamb are best saved for a cruelty-free treat.

££-£££
Vegan
Some Gluten Free

Notting Hill

Restaurants, Cafés & Bars:

1) Farmacy
2) Juicebaby
3) Redemption

Shops:

Farmacy ❶
INTERNATIONAL FINE DINING
74 Westbourne Grove, W2 5SH
Tel: 020 7221 0705
www.farmacylondon.com
Insta: @farmacyuk
Travel: Bayswater/Royal Oak LU
Open: Mon-Fri 9am-5pm & 6pm-10pm,
Sat 9am-4pm & 6pm-10pm, Sun 9am-4pm & 6pm-9.30pm

Tied with Vanilla Black for London's most expensive pure vegetarian and vegan eatery, Farmacy certainly has the look and feel of the kind of classy, high-end restaurant that you would expect in this neck of the woods. The rustic tables and chic minimalist chairs wrap around a 360 degrees bar, and the whole space is teeming with lush plant-life.

The food is on-trend and makes full use of 'health-bringing' ingredients like Tigernut milk and probiotics, but the delivery of dishes like nachos and salad is relatively standard. They offer bowls, burgers and breakfasts too, presented attractively, but in small portions. These come with a higher price tag than you will pay at other places, with avocado and egg on toast costing £12. Their puddings and pancakes won't leave a bad taste in your mouth however – they satisfy all those sweet cravings while being dairy, refined sugars and additives free. A filling breakfast will likely set you back £20, and if you're dining here in the evening and drink alcohol, then expect to set aside at least £50 per person. Farmacy may be expensive, but they do offer a welcome opportunity for vegans and vegetarians to enjoy luxury dining in a completely meat and dairy free setting.

£££
Vegetarian & Vegan
Gluten Free
Raw

Juicebaby ❷
VEGAN, GLUTENFREE AND RAW CAFÉ
181 Westbourne Grove, W11 2SB
Tel: 020 7221 2144
Travel: Notting Hill Gate LU
www.juicebaby.co.uk
Twitter/Insta: @juicebabyuk
Open: Mon-Fri 7.30am-7pm, Sat 8am-7pm,
Sun 8am-6pm

Juicebaby is a welcome addition to west London high streets, offering a healthy, vegan, 'clean-eating' kitchen with plenty of take-out options. Their philosophy is all about substituting the bad for the deceptively good, and they've pulled it off with their organic juices, salad bowls, acai and sweet treats. The place to eat if you want to feel naughty but not nasty, as their goods are all carefully made, as unprocessed as possible and without any of those troublesome ingredients – gluten, refined sugars and chemical preservatives. The shops are both laid out similarly, with lots of comfy benches and tables to enjoy your food, and 'positive' slogans adorning the walls. Prices are especially reasonable for a clean-eating Kensington eatery, and you can expect to slurp or munch down a meal here for around £10, with most lunch options costing around £7, and drinks and snacks for less. Juicebaby is a good option if you're looking for healthy food in a fashionable but relaxed atmosphere.

Branch at:
398 Kings Road, SW10 0LJ, see p.152

£-££
Vegan
Gluten Free
Raw

Redemption ❸
VEGAN, GLUTEN-FREE AND RAW CAFÉ
6 Chepstow Road, W2 5BH
Tel: 020 7313 9041
www.redemptionbar.co.uk
Insta: @redemptionbar
Travel: Notting Hill Gate LU
Open: Tues-Sat 12noon-10.30pm, Sun 10am-5pm

Redemption serves cruelty-free health foods in its two London outposts. Both venues offer a fashionable but comfortable environment and are worth a visit, not least for their excellent 'grown up' mocktails. Stone table-tops and ambient lighting make for an attractive setting, equally suitable for cool lunch breaks or cosy dinner dates.

The food is diverse, tasty and healthy, with burgers and risotto bowls sitting alongside sushi roll platters and curries on the menu. There are lots of raw options and all the dishes are vegan and free from wheat and refined sugar. The prices are competitive given the fashionable locations with mains capping at £14 (and plenty for less), and alcohol-free drinks starting at £4. If you're committed to clean-eating or just curious, Redemption makes being healthy as far from a chore as possible. It's a great place for a meal and drink out without feeling weighed down or regretting it the next day.

Branch at:
320 Old Street, EC1V 9DR, see p.304

££
Vegan
Some Gluten Free and Raw

Richmond

Restaurants, Cafés & Bars:

1) Bhuti
2) Hollyhock Café
3) Tide Tables Café
4) The Retreat Kitchen

Bhuti Café ❶
VEGAN, GLUTEN-FREE AND RAW CAFÉ

50 Hill Rise, TW10 6UB
Tel: 033 0400 3108
www.bhuti.co
Twitter/Insta: @bhutilondon
Travel: Richmond LU/LO/Rail
Open: Mon-Fri 8am-9pm, Sat-Sun 8am-7pm

Much in keeping with the tranquil, almost retreat-like atmosphere of Richmond, Bhuti is a 'wellness' centre offering yoga classes and therapeutic treatments, and also boasts a pretty good café too. All the food is vegan, organic, gluten and refined sugar free, and prepared with a commitment to keeping it as healthy as possible. There's a selective all-day brunch menu, as well as a few varieties of build-your-own salad bowls on offer, plus some snacks and 'health-bringing' beverages to boot. For brunch, you can expect porridge, granola, pancakes and avo' on toast, and with the salads you'll be spoilt for choice.

Bhuti also offers more substantial options like roasted veggies, falafels and bean burgers. If you do fancy washing this down with something, then expect spiced lattes, liquid food juices and 'mylks' aplenty. Prices are reasonable with brunch options for £5 to £8 and main meals for £9 to £12. The minimalism of the eating space is refreshing – sleek wooden furniture, visible kitchen space and only a couple of mandalas in sight. Bhuti Café is a great option for anyone looking for an affordable, healthy eatery in the area.

£-££
Vegan
Gluten Free
Raw

Hollyhock Café ❷
HOMEMADE CAFÉ STAPLES
Terrace Gardens, TW10 6UX
www.tidetablescafe.co.uk
Tel: 020 8948 6555

TideTables ❸
HOMEMADE CAFÉ STAPLES
2 The Arches, TW9 1TH
www.tidetablescafe.co.uk
Tel: 020 8948 8285

Twitter: @TideTablesCafé
Travel: Richmond LU/LO
Open: Mon-Fri 8.30am-6.30pm, Sat-Sun 8.30am-8pm
These sister cafés in Richmond are charming spots to enjoy vegetarian food with a view. You can choose between looking onto the river from a large, tree-covered outdoor space and archway, or in a rustic cottage surrounded by the Terrace Gardens. Both serve homely vegetarian and vegan food like pies, lasagne and salad, and only make use of fair trade and organic produce. If you just want a snack they also have a range of beers, hot drinks and pastries. Prices are very fair, with filling mains costing around £5 to £6, and lighter options for a lot less. Though on the outskirts of London, these cafés merit a visit because of their idyllic locations in Richmond, and are surrounded by plenty of things to do and see while there too.

£
Vegetarian
Vegan
some Gluten Free and Raw

Hollyhock Café

The Retreat Kitchen ❹

CAFÉ STAPLES

16 Hill Rise, TW10 6UA
Tel: 020 8127 0700
www.theretreatkitchen.co.uk
Twitter:@retreatkitchen/Insta: @theretreatkitchen
Travel: Richmond LU/LO/Rail
Open: Mon-Fri 8.30am-5pm, Sat-Sun 9am-5pm

TV star Nick Knowles, inspired by his BBC & Netflix series The Retreat, has co-opened The Retreat Kitchen in Richmond as a way of promoting a healthier way of living. Its plant-based offering is comprehensive, with breakfasts, brunches and lunches available for both the sweet and savoury toothed. Everything is homemade and organic, dishes include a full English breakfast, omelettes, berry bowls, salads, and wraps. They also serve more hot drinks, smoothies and juices than you can shake a stick at.

The Retreat Kitchen supports businesses that dually operate as social enterprises, such the Old Spike Roastery, who use their profits from coffee production to help the homeless. The Retreat's cakes are large, fruity affairs that after a slice will leave you wishing you could take the whole thing home. As a health food and plant-based eatery goes, The Retreat Kitchen is reasonably and competitively priced. Whether you're on a trip to Richmond, or a local passing by, pop into The Retreat Kitchen for some good food and drink and time well spent.

£
Vegan

SOUTH

Balham
Wicked Vegan
VEGAN AMERICAN DINER
14 Hildreth Street, SW12 9RQ
www.wickedvegan.uk
Insta: wickedveganuk
Open: Tues-Sat 11am-9pm, Sun 11am-6pm

Balham has been something of a vegan desert until the arrival of Wicked Vegan who have converted an ordinary shop into a smart open fronted diner complete with lots of outdoor seating on fine days. The décor is chic urban industrial with blackboard menus, simple wood tables and a stainless steel clad kitchen where you can see your chosen dish being prepared. The main draw here are the vegan burgers with four patties to choose from, served with a range of toppings, salads and relishes and encased in a freshly toasted bun. The portions are generous and with a selection of fries and sides there is enough here to satisfy the heartiest of appetites. Not every vegan relishes the idea of a burger and for those who want to try something different there is a small but tasty selection of baps, wraps and specials including the delicious Fooled Pork Wrap and the always reliable Mac & Cheese. If all this rich indulgent vegan fast food doesn't leave you satisfied there are also a few sweet treats to round off the meal including moreish flapjacks and generous slices of raspberry & Chocolate cake. The friendly counter service and laid-back vibe, complete with Motown soundtrack, make this a great place to relax, fill your boots and watch the world go by. A great new addition to London's vegan landscape and, judging by the full tables and busy take-out service, one destined to stick around.

££
Vegan
Some Gluten Free

Brixton

Restaurants, Cafés & Bars:

1) Alkaline
2) Blank Brixton
3) Eat of Eden
4) KATAKATA
5) Ms Cupcake
6) Oracles Organic

Shops:

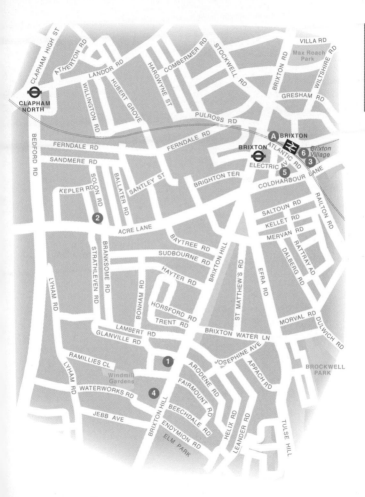

Alkaline Brixton ❶

CARIBBEAN AND JUICE BAR

100b Brixton Hill SW2 1AH
Tel: 020 8678 6900
Insta: @alkalinecleanse
Travel: Brixton LU
Open: Mon-Sat 8am-7pm, Sun 10am-6pm

This teeny little spot might be discreetly wedged onto a corner of Brixton Hill, but if passing by it's not one to miss. Alkaline is a juice bar cum café that serve juices and street food meals with the finest of vegan, organic produce. With unusual ingredients like bluggoe, burdock, fonio and cacao, there is some serious plant-based power and vitality in Alkaline's goodies.

Salad boxes, raw cakes and stews can all be enjoyed alongside the plethora of drinks on offer. Most things cost between £3 and £5, making this an affordable place to eat, particularly versus the other 'clean-eating' restaurants to be found out West. You might have to compete over the narrow counters and stools, but most of the local health-conscious crowd who make a regular pilgrimage through Alkaline's doors are using the take-away service. Alkaline has acquired something of a reputation in Brixton and there are often queues but their fresh juices are worth the wait.

£
Vegan
Some Gluten Free and Raw

Blank Brixton ❷
CAFÉ STAPLES
144 Acre Lane, SW2 5UT
Tel: 077 8860 2119
Insta: @blankbrixton
Travel: Brixton LU/Clapham North LU
Open: Mon-Fri 7am-5pm, Sat-Sun 8am-5pm

Blank is the latest addition to Brixton's vegan scene. A 100% plant-based café that claims to offer the area's best coffee and food, a confidence that is borne out on their Instagram account. Café affogato's ooze ice cream over the brim of the glass and meatless sausage rolls offer a substantial snack.

Of course, you can always opt for a healthy vegan scramble of mushrooms, tomatoes and avocado and a regular coffee. If good food isn't enough, they also offer regular yoga classes, a play area for kids and cinema showings in their basement. Exposed brick walls, pendant lighting and smooth wooden furnishings give a trendy touch to this down-to-earth spot, where an artisanal coffee costs just £2.50 and meals between £5 and £7. Blanks may be a little off the main Brixton drag, but it's worth seeking out for the great food and friendly service.

£
Vegan

Eat of Eden ❸
CARIBBEAN
Unit 4 Brixton Village
Coldharbour Lane, SW9 8PS
Tel: 020 7737 7566
www.eatofeden.co.uk
Insta: @eat_of_eden
Travel: Brixton LU
Open: Mon 11am-6pm, Tues-Sun 11am-10pm

Eat of Eden is a long-established feature of Brixton Village. It's a laid-back diner serving great Caribbean curries that are rich in legumes and other hearty veg. They offer plenty of patties featuring favourite fillings like callaloo and a host of other easy to eat West Indian foods like macaroni pie, dumplings and plantain. Everything on offer is vegan, meaning you can do away with the often meaty menus of other Caribbean kitchens and enjoy Eat of Eden guilt-free.

If the cuisine is new to you, there are sharing platters for one or two, but if you feel safer sticking to something you know, the burgers and wraps are very tasty. Eat Eden's drinks are just as varied, with Guinness punch sitting side by side with herbal & fruit teas. Prices are reasonable, with all their single dishes costing no more than £5 and there are plenty of seats, both inside and out. Eat of Eden is a no-frills eatery but the food is excellent and the portions generous, making this a great choice when you're visiting Brixton and its markets.

£-££
Vegan
Some Gluten Free

KATAKATA ❹
FRENCH GALETTES AND CREPES
132 Brixton Hill, SW2 1RS
Tel: 020 3490 1160 or 0793 252 7121
Twitter/Insta: @katakatabrixton
Travel: Brixton LU
Open: Daily 10am-10pm

A cheap eat can always be found at KATAKATA. It's a vegetarian café with plenty of vegan options, situated among a number of salt of the earth eateries that represent what Brixton is all about. Alongside the workshops they run on healthy living and the art and music events they host, you can enjoy French galettes, crêpes and fresh juices here for a lot cheaper than most of the chain restaurants down the road. Choose between cheesy buckwheat pancakes or vegan alternatives, and fill up with jerk tofu and a tonne of veg too. All galettes come with a carrot, bean shoot, beetroot and spinach salad that is both tasty and filling. A juice and galette combo is just £5, so ditch the supermarket meal deal and get yourself some real food.

£
Vegetarian
Some Gluten Free
Some Vegan

Ms Cupcake ❺

VEGAN BAKERY
408 Coldharbour Lane, SW9 8LF
Tel: 020 3086 8933
www.mscupcake.co.uk
Travel: Brixton LU
Open: Sun-Wed 10am-7pm, Thurs-Sat 10am-8pm

This humble Brixton bakery is popular for the range of cupcakes and other sweet treats it serves which are rich with brightly coloured icing, tasty and all vegan. This is London's first vegan bakery and the eponymous Ms Cupcake has become a semi celebrity, having published her own cookbook and made TV appearances.

With an unhealthy selection of flavours to try out, from Jaffa cake to Bakewell tart, the best thing about this place is mixing and matching the different baked goods and having fun. There are special deals for the more you buy too, making this a good option when buying treats for friends and family. Otherwise, the prices are around or a little above average, at about £3 per item. If you don't fancy something sweet, then they sell sandwiches too, but there is only limited outdoor seating and Ms Cupcake is largely set up as a delivery/take away service. All things considered, Ms Cupcake is a sound option when pastries are called for and is providing a great service to London's vegan community.

£
Vegan
Some Gluten Free

Oracles Organic ❻
CARIBBEAN AND JUICE BAR

6th Avenue, Brixton Village, SW9 8PS
Tel: 075 8424 0909
www.oraclesorganics.co.uk
Travel: Brixton LU
Open: Mon 10am-6pm, Tues-Weds 10am-7pm,
Thurs-Sat 10am-10pm, Sun 10.30am-6pm

This Jamaican juice bar and vegan eatery is a good option when on the prowl for healthy, organic fare in Brixton. Offering a range of vegetable and fruit juices, this is the place to come for a shot or two of your five a day, and they make colourful salads, soups and hot meals like curry and stew too. They also double as a small organic vegan grocers, stocking mostly dry goods like peanut butter and quinoa. If eating in, then expect to spend around £5 on juices, £4 on soup or £8 on curry and stew, with things costing a little less to take out. There are a few tables and chairs, both inside and outside the store, and you'll always be under the cover of the Brixton Village roof. Oracles Organic is one of the best, healthiest and purely vegan options in the area, and a must-visit for locals.

£
Vegan
Some Gluten Free and Raw

Brockley

The Broca Café
HOMEMADE CAFÉ STAPLES
3 & 4 Coulgate Street, SE4 2RW
Tel: 020 7277 7888
www.thebroca.com
Twitter:@thebroca / Insta: @thebrocacafe
Travel: Brockley LO
Open: Mon-Fri 7am-7pm, Sat 8am-6pm, Sun 10am-4pm

Brockley might be a part of London that is out of sight for some, but if you ever find yourself fortunate enough to wander out of the station, then Broca is hard to miss. A bright yellow façade captures the eye before you walk in to find a homely local café that was actually the area's first coffeshop.

In the years since its inception, Broca Café has mastered the art of bringing comforting hot drinks, veggie and vegan brunches and plenty more to the crowd that are lucky enough to call this their local. Meatless Full English's, waffles, sandwiches and cakes are all available here, plus artisan coffee and alcoholic beverages too if they take your fancy. The food and drinks are all great value and Broca has lots of outdoor seating for when the weather is fine and a shabby chic interior for when it's chilly. If you need top quality organic groceries, then Broca's also the best go-to in the area, stocking everything from dried and jarred goods to fresh bread and eggs.

£
Vegetarian

Crystal Palace & Sydenham

Made from Plants
PASTRIES, CAKES, SANDWICHES AND HOT DRINKS
120a Anerley Road, SE19 2AN
www.madefromplants.co.uk
Insta: @madefromplantsldn
Travel: Crystal Palace Rail
Open: Thurs-Fri 7am-5pm, Sat-Sun 11am-5pm
This south London gem serves some top homemade vegan
food, both sweet and savoury, out of a small café in Crystal
Palace. A glance at their Instagram shows brioche buns,
sausage rolls, chocolate cakes and stacked up sandwiches, all
of which look (and are) delicious.

You can also enjoy their selection of drinks, which boasts
freshly squeezed juices, smoothies, milkshakes and hot
beverages. The space is small, but many people use the takeaway service, particularly on fine days with Crystal Palace Park
just opposite providing a perfect place for an al fresco lunch.
Cookies start at just 50p, and most things aren't more expensive
than £2.50, and nothing more than £4. Regardless of whether
you're plant-based or not – if you are in the area then Made
From Plants is well worth a visit.

£
Vegan

Deptford & New Cross

The Full Nelson
VEGAN AMERICAN DINER
47 Deptford Broadway, SE8 4PH
www.thefullnelsondeptford.co.uk
Twitter: @FullNelsonSE8 / Insta: @thefullnelsondeptford
Travel: Deptford Bridge DLR / New Cross LO
Open: Mon-Thurs 4pm-10pm, Fri 4pm-11pm,
Sat 12noon-11pm, Sun 11am-4pm

The Full Nelson is like its little brother The Waiting Room (see p.200), a veggie and vegan treasure in south London, where you can enjoy good food and beer for just a few quid. The space itself might be small, but makes up for it with big portions of 'seitanic' wings, stacked up 'beef' burgers with their 'Deptford Death Sauce' and lots of deep fried treats. Everything is vegetarian or can be prepared vegan, and a meal here makes for a welcome change from the health-foods hysteria of many plant-based eateries. Their list of cocktails and craft beers puts many an establishment to shame, and they've got hard shakes and flavoured shots if you're up for a bit of fun. The prices are reasonable with a meal deal of burger, fries and a beer costing just £10. The Full Nelson is cosy but there's enough room across a few wooden benches and tables for groups to make a night of it here. The Full Nelson is a great place to indulge in some meat-free munch accompanied by some excellent beers.

£
Vegetarian
Some Vegan

Hullabaloo
INDIAN VEGETARIAN RESTAURANT
111B Deptford High Street, SE8 4RQ
Tel: 020 7018 4747
www.hullabaloostreetfood.com
Twitter: @hullabaloofood
Insta: @hullabaloostreetfood
Travel: Deptford Rail
Open: Mon-Fri 12noon-3pm & 5-10pm,
Sat-Sun 12noon-3pm & 5-11pm

This Indian street food eatery really feels like a dhaba (roadside eatery in India), serving inexpensive curries in a small room with Bollywood film posters on the walls. The menu is small, with a select few curries that are all clearly labelled as either vegan or vegetarian. It boils down to having mixed vegetable, tofu or paneer curry, all of which are priced at £5.50, and can be enjoyed alongside cheaper classic sides and starters like samosas, saag aloo and daal. The space is a little cramped, and more like a café than a restaurant, but is still worth a visit. Get down to Hullabaloo to see what all the fuss is about – it's a firm favourite with locals seeking authentic Indian fare.

£
Vegetarian
Some Vegan

The Waiting Room
AMERICAN DINER AND CAFÉ STAPLES
142 Deptford High Street, SE8 3PQ
Tel: 020 3601 0100
Twitter/Insta: @waitingroomse8
Travel: Deptford Rail
Open: Mon-Fri 8am-6.30pm, Sat 9am-6.30pm, Sun 10am-4pm

This narrow little café is a friendly spot located towards the end of Deptford Market and which has a loyal following among the locals. The Waiting Room has a friendly vibe with lots of regulars showing up for a chat and their favourite dish from a menu that includes veggie hot dogs and ribs, as well as brunch staples like porridge, pancakes and eggs. The Waiting Room is also rightly proud of its hand-roasted coffee, which they source from Union.

The small space has bags of individuality and quirkiness – assorted posters and wacky statues are all over the place and you'll find books and even VHS' to exchange. The quirkiness extends to the menu including 'Sith Lord Burgers' with 'Deptford Death Sauce' and 'New Yorker' hot dogs with a mug of 'Woody Allen'. As well as being fun and tasty, the food is great value and the portions generous. It's a friendly place to sit and relax but if seating is limited they also do a great take-out service. Their older brother down the road, The Full Nelson (see p.196), is the place to go in the evenings for much of the same top quality vegan and veggie fast food, as well as top beers and cocktails.

£
Vegetarian

East Dulwich

The Blue Brick Café
HOMEMADE CAFÉ STAPLES
14 Fellbrigg Road, SE22 9HH
Tel: 020 8299 8670
www.cargocollective.com/bluebrickcafe
Insta: bluebrickcafe
Travel: East Dulwich Rail
Open: Mon-Sat 9am-5.30pm, Sun 9.30am-5pm

The Blue Brick Café is a charming neighbourhood café in the slightly sleepy heart of south London. The eponymous blue brickwork and classic typography provide the perfect façade to a homely interior that is filled with natural light and a mix of vintage furniture and homewares. It is the perfect brunch location, come rain or shine, and not just for its cosy atmosphere – they know how to do food and drink too.

Everything here is vegetarian or vegan, and uses fresh, seasonal produce and artisan products like Climpson and Sons coffee, belying the premises' past as a greasy spoon. Tasty soups, fragrant salads and spicy stews make up the bulk of their mains menu, but you can also get a comforting bowl of spaghetti or a meat-free fry up if you fancy. They have other breakfast options and a host of great pastries, cakes and desserts. Quality food and drink doesn't come at a premium here, with plentiful breakfasts, brunches or lunches only costing between £5 and £10. We're thoroughly jealous of the citizens of Dulwich who get to call The Blue Brick Café their local – a 5 star London eatery.

£
Vegetarian
Some Vegan

Elephant & Castle, Vauxhall & Lambeth

Restaurants, Cafés & Bars:

1) The Bonnington Café
2) Café at Jamyang
3) Café Van Gogh
4) Cupcake and Shhht
5) The Ragged Canteen

Shops:

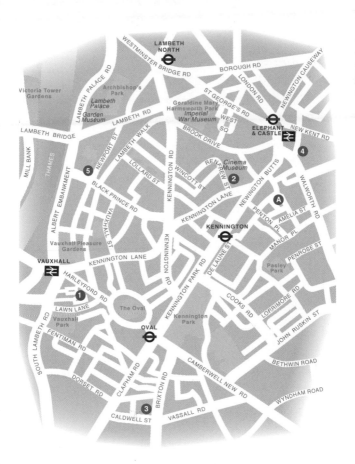

LAMBETH
NORTH

WESTMINSTER BRIDGE RD

BOROUGH RD

NEWINGTON CAUSEWAY

LONDON RD

ST GEORGE'S RD

Victoria Tower
Gardens

Archbishop's
Park

LAMBETH PALACE RD

Lambeth
Palace
Garden
Museum

LAMBETH RD

Geraldine Mary
Harmsworth Park
Imperial
War Museum

WEST
SQ

ELEPHANT
& CASTLE

NEW KENT RD

4

LAMBETH BRIDGE

MILL BANK

THAMES

NEWPORT ST

LAMBETH WALK

BLACK PRINCE RD

LOLLARD ST

BROOK DRIVE

KENNINGTON RD

WINCOTT ST

RENFREW ST

Cinema
Museum

2

NEWINGTON BUTTS

PENTON PL

AMELIA ST

WALWORTH RD

A

5

ALBERT EMBANKMENT

VAUXHALL ST

KENNINGTON LANE

KENNINGTON
MANOR PL

PENROSE ST

Pasley
Park

Vauxhall Pleasure
Gardens

VAUXHALL

KENNINGTON LANE

KENNINGTON RD

KENNINGTON PARK RD

DE LAUNE ST

COOKS RD

LOPRIMORE RD

JOHN RUSKIN ST

HARLEYFORD RD

1

LAWN LANE

Vauxhall
Park

FENTIMAN RD

SOUTH LAMBETH

The Oval

OVAL

Kennington
Park

CAMBERWELL NEW RD

BETHWIN ROAD

WYNDHAM ROAD

DORSET RD

CLAPHAM RD

BRIXTON RD

3

CALDWELL ST

VASSALL RD

The Bonnington Café ❶
INTERNATIONAL VEGETARIAN CAFÉ AND COMMUNITY CENTRE

11 Vauxhall Grove, SW8 1TD
Tel: 075 5247 5535
www.bonningtoncafe.co.uk
Travel: Vauxhall LU
Open: Daily Mon-Sun 12noon-2pm & 6.30pm-11pm

The Bonnington Café and Centre is a special place that we're delighted we can still include in the book, after thousands of petitioners saved it from closure. It resides in the idyllic Bonnington Square and Gardens which is a small enclave of tranquillity that wouldn't be out of place in a British soap opera or film. The centre itself has been serving the local community's needs since the '80's, and welcomes allcomers to its creative and fitness classes and cultural events.

The café shares this history and is run as a cooperative serving vegetarian and vegan food. The chefs take turns to cook here (which can be checked out online), resulting in a 'no-menu' style of service with the food changing depending on the day's chef. This might sound chaotic but the chefs are all experienced and the food always fantastic. We're certain you'll be as pleasantly surprised by the food on offer as by the affordable prices – around £10 can get you a three course meal. Bear in mind they're unlicensed so bring your own bottle (or two, as they don't charge corkage), and make sure to check in advance if they're operating as cash only. In this unpretentious restaurant, evening meals can be enjoyed by candlelight and winter dinners beside the fire. Bonnington Café is an absolute gem and one of our firm favourites.

£
Vegetarian & Vegan
Varied Cuisine – depends on resident chef

Café at Jamyang ❷
VEGETAL CAFÉ
43 Renfrew Road, SE11 4NA
Tel: 020 7820 8787
www.cafeatjamyang.co.uk
Twitter/Insta: @cafeatjamyang
Travel: Kennington LU
Open: Mon-Fri 10am-4pm

Situated behind the Jamyang Buddhist Centre is a café that promotes 'vegetal' food that is sourced locally, organically and from fair-trade suppliers. They focus on freshly made salads, mains and cakes that'll leave you feeling as refreshed as the meditative practice that they are so closely linked with.

Expect to find the dishes ranging from the Levant and South Asia to classic French quiches – it's down to whatever is seasonal and what the chefs are inspired to make on the day. The space is plainly furnished, with a mix of wooden chairs and tables and the garden space, looking onto a golden reclining Buddha statue, makes for a charming summer spot. A main and salad combined is around £7 and everything on the menu is great value. Café at Jamyang is an easy-going vegetarian eatery with vegan options, perfect for when in Kennington or visiting the Jamyang Centre.

£
Vegetarian
Some Vegan

Café van Gogh ❸

INTERNATIONAL VEGAN
88 Brixton Road, SW9 6BE
Tel: 075 4696 6554
www.cafevangogh.co.uk
Twitter: @cafevangoghCIC
Insta: @cafevangogh01
Travel: Oval LU
Open: Tues-Sat 10am-9pm, Sun 12noon-5pm

A local favourite for many, this south London eatery is a charming spot with a ceiling depicting a starry night sky inspired by the eponymous artist. Sitting adjacent to a church in a small, listed brick building, it's an inviting place to enjoy a vegan lunch or dinner with staple dishes and foods inspired by the chef's travels. There are some hearty favourites here like burgers, bangers & mash, dhal and jerk plantain with changing specials that mix it up for seasoned visitors. The portions are generous and everything is reasonably priced, making this a great option if you're in the Oval area.

They also host a blog that posts recipes and recommendations for vegans, particularly focused on making London vegan living a little easier. There's outdoor seating on fine days and for those with dogs, and plenty of space across the two floors, connected by a winding staircase. Café van Gogh is a popular place, so if you're visiting in a group of more than four it's a good idea to book a table to avoid disappointment. It might not be incredibly adventurous in its menu, but this café does everything well and with care, making it well worth a special visit.

£-££
Vegan

Cupcakes and Shhht ❹
DESSERTS AND CAFÉ STAPLES
10 Elephant Road, SE17 1AY
Tel: 075 4598 0977
www.cupcakesandshhht.com
Twitter/Insta: @CupcakesnShhht
Travel: Elephant and Castle LU
Open: Mon-Sat 9am-5pm, Sun 10am-5pm

Cupcakes and Shhht made their first home in a shipping container in Elephant and Castle from which they've been serving a tonnage of over-the-top sweet treats, drinks and a few savoury foods. Sadly, this part of Elephant and Castle is due for redevelopment and so these guys are set to migrate to Hackney later in 2018 (see their website for details). Wherever they land, you'll still be able to rely on their brightly coloured cupcakes, brownies and creamy coffees, all of which are best experienced when combined into freak shakes, which we think are the best in town. They have lots of raw, gluten free and refined sugar free options available on their menu too.

A lot of love, good ingredients (sourced ethically) and skill goes into the making of their products, but all this care comes at a price with freak shakes costing £8 and a vegan 'fry up' £12. You'd probably be wise not to make either of these an everyday indulgence at any rate, but Cupcakes and Shhht is a great place to enjoy delicious vegan desserts. Let's hope they are as successful in their new location.

££
Vegan
Some Gluten Free and Raw

The Ragged Canteen ❺
HOMEMADE CAFÉ STAPLES

Beaconsfield Gallery, 22 Newport Street, SE11 6AY
Tel: 020 7582 6465
www.beaconsfield.ltd.uk/café
Insta: raggedcanteen
Travel: Vauxhall LU
Open: Wed-Sun 11am-5pm

Located in the Beaconsfield Gallery, this artfully minimal space offers vegetarian and vegan brunches, lunches and amazing homemade baked goods that call for a visit in their own right. The passion they have for sourcing their food ethically shows in their daily changing seasonal menu, that also has plenty of gluten-free options.

The Ragged Canteen makes an effort to source foods from local urban growers and foragers. These are used to create colourful dishes that take their inspiration from around the world, as can be seen on the Canteen's Instagram account. You can expect to find salads, sandwiches and specials that taste as good as they look. Despite all this effort, the prices are very reasonable and the canteen has a loyal following among local office workers. Expect to spend around £6 or £7 for a good brunch or lunch, and less for an exceptionally good coffee and cake. The Ragged Canteen is part of the Beaconsfield Gallery and eating here is a great opportunity to catch up on the gallery's changing programme of events and exhibitions. With free Wi-Fi and a terrace for the summer, the only thing this eatery is free of is meat, so for veggies, vegans and the curious alike, be sure to schedule a visit.

£
Vegetarian + Vegan
Some Gluten Free and Raw

Peckham

Restaurants, Cafés & Bars:

1) 2 Girls' Café
2) Deserted Cactus
3) LEVELSIX Yoga Café
4) Persepolis and Snackistan
5) PickyWops
6) Wildflower
7) Zionly Manna

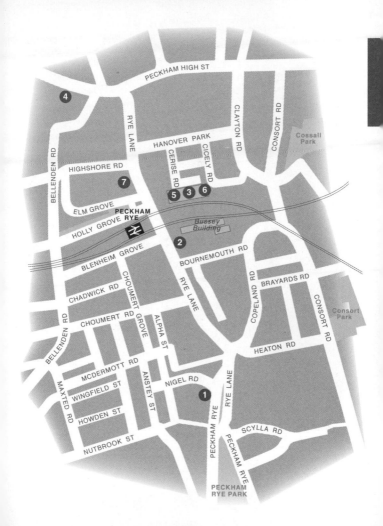

PECKHAM HIGH ST

④

Cossall
Park

RYE LANE

BELLENDEN RD

CLAYTON RD

CONSORT RD

HANOVER PARK

HIGHSHORE RD

CERISE RD

CICELY RD

⑦

⑤ ③ ⑥

ELM GROVE

PECKHAM
RYE

HOLLY GROVE

Buesey
Building

②

BLENHEIM GROVE

BOURNEMOUTH RD

CHADWICK RD

CHOUMERT GROVE

RYE LANE

COPELAND RD

BRAYARDS RD

CHOUMERT RD

BELLENDEN RD

MAXTED RD

ALPHA ST

CONSORT RD

Consort
Park

MCDERMOTT RD

HEATON RD

WINGFIELD ST

ANSTEY ST

NIGEL RD

HOWDEN ST

①

RYE LANE

NUTBROOK ST

PECKHAM RYE

SCYLLA RD

PECKHAM RYE

PECKHAM
RYE PARK

2 Girls' Café ❶
HOMEMADE CAFÉ STAPLES
24a Peckham Rye, SE15 4JR
Tel: 077 5343 2163
Insta: /2girls_cafe
Open: Mon-Fri 9am-5pm, Sat 10am-5pm, Sun 9am-5pm

This cosy little café is one of Peckham's hidden gems. The two girls in question, Anna and Kinga, offer a great selection of homemade foods, wonderful vegan cakes and sweet treats and a bewildering list of teas, coffees and smoothies including intriguingly named Beetroot Power and Pink Coconut. The menu includes Buddha bowls, spicy tacos and substantial bean burritos with the scrambled tofu on sourdough with avocado, tomato and spring onion one of our firm favourites.

Everything on the menu is vegan and there are lots of gluten-free options, including delicious sweet treats like the freshly made peanut butter bar. The café also has a small zero waste shop which offers beans and pulses and other dry goods, all sold by weight with customers bringing their own containers to minimise packaging. In addition the back room often hosts exhibitions by local artists and other occasional events. This gem of a café is a welcome break from the hectic environment of Peckham Rye and just a short walk from the award-winning greenery of Peckham Rye Park.

£
Vegan
Some Gluten Free and Raw

Deserted Cactus ❷
CARIBBEAN

Holdron's Arcade, Unit 23 & 25 135A Peckham Rye, SE15 4ST
Insta: @deserted_cactus
Travel: Peckham Rye LO
Open: Tues-Fri 1pm-4pm, Sat 1pm-7pm

You'll be hard-pressed to find a hole in the wall serving vegan grub as good as Deserted Cactus, even with the changes that Peckham and Holdron's Arcade are going through. Bowls full of the best of Afro-Caribbean cooking are available throughout much of the week, such as butterbean curries and pumpkin stews.

They also offer trays of mac'n'cheese and tubs of southern fried jackfruit if you want something filling but not too spicy. Though £8-£10 seems steep for lunch, the loyal customers here will testify it's worth every penny. There isn't much in the way of seating, so anticipate enjoying this standing up or on the go. And the owner Esme – known also as London Afro Vegan – has a fantastic, eponymous YouTube channel with videos covering everything from recipes to shopping hauls.

£
Vegan
Some Gluten Free

LEVELSIX Yoga Café ③

HEALTHFOODS

Floor 6, Peckham Levels,
95a Rye Lane, Peckham, SE15 4TG
Tel: 020 3941 1950
www.levelsixstudios.co.uk
Insta: @levelsixpeckam
Open: Mon-Sat 8am-3pm

This café is part of the LEVELSIX Yoga Studios and on the walls above the dining area are photos of some of their teachers in various postures. Just opposite, divided by a glass partition, is one of the exercise studios, so occasional sounds of 'Ohm' fill the café. Despite its unlikely location, LEVELSIX's café is a tranquil spot but hidden away within the busy hub of Peckham Levels.

The café is run with an ethos of health and sustainability, using almost exclusively organic produce. The daily menu offers flavourful, nourishing dishes along with a range of freshly prepared juices and smoothies from an ever changing seasonal menu. Expect to find delicious breakfasts such as 'epic' almond milk and chia seed porridge, complete with a range of toppings including goji jam and toasted coconut chips. There is also a small but carefully prepared list of lunch dishes whether you're after a hearty salad, a daily soup with seeded loaf or the house special, home-made satay sauce and plaintain, topped with toasted tamari seeds. The menu is devised and prepared by head chef Woody Pyke, who is committed to using locally sourced produce wherever possible and to a menu that is mainly vegan and gluten free. Although primarily used by members of this busy yoga studio, it offers a warm welcome to all.

£
Vegan
Some Gluten Free

Persepolis and Snackistan ❹
MIDDLE EASTERN CAFÉ AND DELI
28-30 Peckham High Street, SE15 5DT
Tel: 020 7639 8007
www.foratasteofpersia.co.uk
Twitter: @PersiainPeckham
Travel: Peckham Rye Station
Open: Daily 10.35am-9pm

You could be forgiven for walking past Persepolis and dismissing it as a just another corner shop. But hidden behind the façade is an establishment that encapsulates Peckham's diversity. A Persian grocery store cum-diner called 'Snackistan', the latter is an essential visit for anybody visiting the area. The interior of the shop is a strange mix of beautifully woven rugs alongside kitschy knick-knacks and shop goods. As quaint as it is queer, the décor is however definitely secondary to the food at Snackistan.

Mezzes make up the menu here, but the options are surprisingly varied and can include falafels, tabboulehs and hummus, all expertly enlivened with the addition of pomegranates, juniper and tahini. The portions are generous and despite the food's light and fresh nature, you can expect to enjoy a substantial meal for around £10. With vegan and gluten-free options and a strictly vegetarian policy, this is a place definitely worth a special visit. Be sure to check out the proprietor Sally Butcher's great cookbooks and store goods, which are a must have for anybody hoping to recreate her magic at home. Sally is usually on hand preparing the food, so if you're lucky you might be able to pickup a signed copy.

£
Vegetarian
Some Vegan
Some Gluten Free

PickyWops ❺

Peckham Levels, Unit 506, 95a Rye Lane, SE15 4ST

Full review see page 146

Wildflower ❻

INTERNATIONAL

Peckham Levels, Level 5, 95a Rye Lane, SE15 4ST

Tel: 020 3735 3775

www.wildflowerpeckham.uk

Twitter: @wildflowerse15 / Insta: @wildflowerpeckham

Travel: Peckham Rye Overground and Rail

Open: Mon, Thurs and Sun 10am-5pm

Tues-Weds, Fri-Sat 10am-9.30pm

Wildflower makes beautiful food and is an Instagrammer's dream. Part of the Peckham Levels group, they're situated in a converted multi-storey car park, and offer a standard of vegan and vegetarian dining that is rarely matched. Using only fresh produce, they make classic brunch dishes, as well as others inspired by Middle Eastern, Asian and Mediterranean cuisine that would put many an indigenous restaurant to shame. They've got plenty of pastries and sweet treats too, all homemade, that are the perfect accompaniment to an impromptu coffee and catch-up. With lots of natural light and plenty of seating, the space is fashionably decorated with industrial fittings of old, minimalist detailing and plenty of leafy houseplants. Wildflower is a great destination for an evening dinner date when the lights cast the room in a cosy red glow, and the place also doubles as a night time music venue, called Ghost Notes, playing mostly jazz. Homemade pastries and snacks cost between £3 and £4, while brunch and dinner mains are between £5 and £9 for plentiful plates of gourmet grub. Wildflower is a real treat and one well worth going out of your way to visit.

£

Vegetarian

Zionly Manna ❼
CARIBBEAN

Zionly Manna Unit 41, Rye Lane Indoor Market, SE15 5BY
Tel: 0783 113 6705
Insta: @zionlymanna
Travel: Peckham Rye LO and Rail
Open: Mon-Sat 10am-6pm

Nestled inside Rye Lane indoor market, you'll find a restaurant that captures the soul of Peckham. Zionly Manna is a vegan eatery that serves Caribbean dishes made in-house by the Rastafarian chef owner Jahson Peat. He cooks daily changing specials of curries, stews and vegetable salads, as well as staples like dumpling and meat-free mutton curry. You can also get some more on-trend options like falafel, liquid food juices and raw kale salads. Root beers, teas and tonics, as well as a range of cakes and other desserts, are available for just a couple of quid. Here, the plates are plentiful and you can get a mountain of comforting vegan grub for around £6, or try a bit of everything for £8. The space is a little ramshackle, with only a few random chairs and tables dotted around the small hole-in-the-wall shop, but the food makes up for the decor. Zionly Manna offers top quality and authentic vegan Caribbean cuisine that beats the chain restaurants serving a poor imitation of these dishes. If you're in Peckham this is definitely one to seek out.

£
Vegan

South Norwood & Croydon

Coffee Shotter

CAFÉ STAPLES
71 High Street, CR0 1QE
www.coffeeshotter.co.uk
Insta: @coffeeshotter
Travel: East/West Croydon Rail
Open: Mon-Fri 7.30am-5pm, Sat 10am-3pm, Sun Closed

Croydon is undergoing a transformation, with a new Westfield shopping centre and developers moving in with plans for new housing developments, but not all of this is at the expense of local residents. Coffee Shotter is a youthful vegetarian café on the high street that serves healthy and affordable plant-based meals, as well as good quality coffee and indulgent pastries.

Most notably, they've channelled the trend of using syringes as an interactive part of the meal – here with donut fillers – to amusing effect. Flavours like Crunchy Bar and Ferrero Rocher can be injected along with caramel and chocolate sauces. Coffee costs between £1.50 and £2.50, and food and pastries between £3 and £6. At present, food is limited to pre-packed meals made by Laura's Idea, who have been supplying local businesses with ready-to-eat meals such as tortilla, calzone and curries for the last 30 years. The space is trendily decorated, making for a welcome change to the chicken shops that otherwise adorn the area.

£
Vegetarian

Communitea Café
MIDDLE EASTERN

80 High Street, SE25 6EA
Tel: 020 8916 1923
www.yallahub.co.uk/communitea
Travel: Norwood Junction Rail
Open: Mon-Weds 8am-6pm, Fri 8am-6pm,
Sat 9am-6pm, Sun 10am-6pm

This local spot in Croydon is part and parcel of Yalla Hub, a community initiative that fosters migrant women's opportunities by giving them employment in this vegetarian eatery. As well as a couple of café breakfast staples, like bagels stuffed with cream cheese, peanut butter and jam, and fruity granola, they serve classic Middle Eastern dishes such as baba ghanoush and grilled vegetable pittas, that are as affordable as they are healthy. Communitea Café also boasts an impressive array of teas to try alongside homemade cakes and other sweet treats. Meals are reasonably priced between £3 and £5 with lighter options and drinks for less. A welcome addition to Croydon's high street, Communitea Café is a lovely spot to eat, and one with an important social mission.

£
Vegetarian

Branch

What the Pitta!
VEGAN KEBAB
Boxpark Croydon, Unit 9, 99 George Street, CR0 1LD
www.whatthepitta.com
Full review, see page 93

Southwark

Tibits
INTERNATIONAL VEGETARIAN BUFFET
124 Southwark Street, SE1 0SW
Tel: 020 7202 8370
www.tibits.co.uk
Twitter: @tibits_uk/ Insta: tibits_restaurants
Travel: Southwark LU
Open: Mon-Wed 7.30am-10pm, Thur-Fri 7.30am-11pm,
Sat 11.30am-11pm, Sun 11.30am-10pm

This Swiss chain has opened stores in Southwark and Mayfair, offering a stylish space to enjoy good vegetarian and vegan salads and mezzes. It's all self-service and pay-by-weight, meaning it needn't be heavy on your wallet unless you zealously fill your plate – expect to pay between £7 and £12. Available to take away or eat in, Tibits makes for a speedy, informal, yet chic, lunch or dinner. There are plenty of options to satisfy a wide variety of tastes and dietary requirements – quinoa salads sit side by side with dahls and battered jalapenos. The majority of the food is light, fresh and healthy, but if you fancy indulging a bit more, they also offer desserts, pastries and alcohol. As buffets go, Tibits is definitely one of Vegan and Veggie London's best.

Branch: 12-14 Heddon Street, W1B 4DA, see page 50

Vegetarian & Vegan
Some Gluten Free and Raw

Branch

by Chloe
One Tower Bridge, 6 Duchess Walk, SE1 2SD
www.eatbychloe.com
Full review see page 36

Streatham

Vegan Express
HEALTH FOODS RESTAURANT AND CATERER
913 Garratt Lane, SW17 0LT
Tel: 020 8127 6560
www.veganexpress.co.uk
Twitter: @express_vegan
Insta: @vogan.express
Travel: Tooting Broadway LU
Open: Tues-Sun 12noon-11pm

'Vegan Express' is a little misleading, suggesting a fast food outlet when this restaurant, located on an unassuming row of local shops in Wandsworth, has far greater ambitions for their business and the food they serve. The chef and owners (Charles and Ulrika) are newcomers to meat-free cuisine, but have evidently learnt quickly. This is helped by the fact that head chef Charles has years of experience working in some of London's most prestigious restaurants. He brings this skill and know-how to his own vegan menu, managing to conjure up delicious vegan interpretations of fish and chips and bangers and mash. The mushroom gravy served here is unctuous, delicious and could match any meat based alternative.

Vegan Express might be a trek for many Londoners, but it's worth the effort with a reasonably priced menu and a well chosen vegan wine list making a meal here a truly memorable experience. This new restaurant might not be well known yet, but is already one of the best vegan restaurants to be found in the capital.

££
Vegan

Wholemeal Café
HOMEMADE CAFÉ STAPLES
1 Shrubbery Roadd, SW16 2AS
Tel: 020 8769 2423
www.wholemealcafe.com
Travel: Streatham Hill Rail/Tooting Bec LU
Open: Daily 12noon-10pm

The Wholemeal Café is a dated veggie and vegan diner serving salads and hot dishes throughout the week, in much the same way it's been doing since it opened in the late 70s. Tucked around the corner from the bustle of Streatham's high street, this south London eatery is plainly furnished in pine, giving the place a distinct no-thrills atmosphere.

Their home-cooked food offers a range of classic dishes like ratatouille, Thai curry and casserole, but their Homity and Banoffee pies are definitely firm favourites with the regulars. Wholemeal Café may not have changed very much over the years, but there is a comfort to be found in this old-fashioned and homely diner. The people here are friendly, the coffee is strong and their traditional pies with custard are a delicious treat. Probably not worth going out of your way to visit, but definitely a good and reliable choice if you're visiting Streatham.

£-££
Vegetarian

Wimbledon

Amrutha Lounge
INDIAN AND THAI BUFFET
326 Garratt Lane, SW18 4EJ
Tel: 079 5754 0666
www.amrutha.co.uk
Travel: Southfields/ Wimbledon Park LU
Open: Tue-Fri 12noon-3.30pm & 6pm-9pm,
Sat 12noon-9pm, Sun 1pm-9pm

This new vegan buffet brings great value food to the meat-free crowd in the area. It boasts a growing menu of healthy Indian and Thai curries and some sweet drinks and treats too.

Expect your much loved creamy coconut flavours and aromatic spices from the kitchen here. Prices are kept low, with the buffet service costing just £10 and smaller plates available (like pakoras and wraps), or sweet things like brownie and cheesecake, for under £5. The interior is plain but pleasant, though you might struggle to fit large parties in here. Amrutha Lounge is a relaxed buffet eatery where you can enjoy some inexpensive and tasty Asian food.

£
Vegan

EAST

Plates

Bethnal Green & Mile End

Restaurants, Cafés & Bars:

1) 90° MELT
2) Antonio's Vegan Italian Kitchen
3 The Canary
4) The Gallery Café
5) Just FaB
6) Sazzy & Fran Café

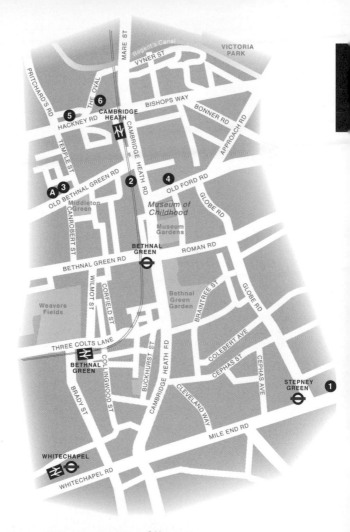

VICTORIA PARK

Regent's Canal

MARE ST

VYNER ST

BISHOPS WAY

BONNER RD

APPROACH RD

PRITCHARD'S RD

THE OVAL

⑥

⑤

CAMBRIDGE HEATH

HACKNEY RD

CAMBRIDGE HEATH RD

TEMPLE ST

OLD BETHNAL GREEN RD

Ⓐ③

②

④

OLD FORD RD

CANROBERT ST

Middleton
Green

*Museum of
Childhood*

GLOBE RD

Museum
Gardens

**BETHNAL
GREEN**

ROMAN RD

BETHNAL GREEN RD

WILMOT ST

CORFIELD ST

Weavers
Fields

Bethnal
Green
Garden

BRAINTREE ST

GLOBE RD

THREE COLTS LANE

**BETHNAL
GREEN**

COLLINGWOOD ST

BUCKHURST ST

CAMBRIDGE HEATH RD

COLEBERT AVE

CEPHAS ST

CEPHAS AVE

BRADY ST

CLEVELAND WAY

**STEPNEY
GREEN**

❶

MILE END RD

WHITECHAPEL

WHITECHAPEL RD

241

90°MELT ❶
VEGGIE AMERICAN DINER
235 Mile End Road, E1
Tel: 020 3754 5711
www.90degreemelt.co.uk
Twitter/ Insta: @90degreemelt
Travel: Stepney Green LU
Open: Mon-Sat 10am-10pm, Sun 11am-4pm

This newcomer to the E1 eating scene is a top treat. An American 'dude food' diner, 90° MELT specialises in grilled cheese melts and 'meaty' burgers, hot dogs and wings. Everything is vegetarian, and nearly all of this can be enjoyed as a vegan or gluten-free option too. If you don't fancy anything from their all-day menu, then weekend brunch offers both classic and nu-age diner food, like pancakes or Shakshuka eggs. Their devious desserts might be dirty for the heart, but are worth it – think over-the-top, fruit-filled pies and brownies.

A veggie or vegan brunch or lunch here needn't be expensive – despite their relatively niche offering, prices range between £4 and £9. They offer alcohol if you want to wash down a meal with something stronger, and many of the familiar American beers feature on the menu. The space is casual and orients around social eating, with long communal benches meaning you won't come here for an intimate eat. We're excited about 90° MELT – this is really an inexpensive and easy place to enjoy dirty vegetarian and vegan food from a cuisine that is all too often restricted to carnivores.

£
Vegetarian
Some Gluten Free

Antonio's Vegan Italian Kitchen ❷

393 Cambridge Heath Road, E2 9RA
Tel: 020 3305 9029
www.antoniosvegankitchen.co.uk
Insta: @antoniosvegankitchen
Travel: Cambridge Heath LO/Bethnal Green LU
Open: Daily 12noon-10pm

As if the name didn't give it away already, Antonio's is a
restaurant where plant-based pastas and pizzas are to be
found on an otherwise plain street in East London. But their
cooking is anything but plain. You needn't look further for
bread and butter Italian cuisine. Stylishly presented Piadina
flatbreads and vegetable antipasto make for authentic starters,
and mains of fresh pasta are served simply, attractively and
full of quality ingredients. Pasta made in house is becoming
something of a rarity in many contemporary Italian kitchens, but
this distinctive aspect to Antonio's preparation comes without
a hint of pretension. You'll find him bedecked in his trilby toiling
away behind the counter, tirelessly hand rolling out classics
like spinach and ricotta Ravioli, truffle Tagliatelle or Lasagne
Bolognese, none of which suffer from feeling vegan. You'd be
forgiven for forgetting why these dishes could need meat at
all – the hallmark of fantastic plant-based cooking. Inexpensive
espressos and a treat of a tiramisu are the recommended ways
to round off a meal here, which will cost between £8.50 and
£11.50 for mains, and a lot less for sides, drinks and desserts.
The restaurant itself is spacious and smart, and open from noon
till night. It's one of the best places to enjoy a hearty lunch or
dinner date for vegans and vegetarians. They're currently Bring-
Your-Own Bottle, but are looking to acquire a licence soon.

Vegan
Some Gluten Free

The Canary ❸
HAIRDRESSERS AND VEGETARIAN CAFÉ

61-63 Old Bethnal Green Road, E2 6QA
Tel: 020 8257 8170
www.thecanary.co.uk
Insta: @thecanary2
Travel: Bethnal Green LU
Open: Tues-Fri 8.30am-8pm, Sat 9.30am-8pm,
Sun 9.30am-6pm

The Canary is a trendy yet inviting hair salon-cum-veggie café that serves Cast Iron Coffee along with cakes, pastries and daily changing specials, all cooked up in a gourmet style by their in-house chef. Vegan and gluten-free options are available among the soups, sandwiches and salads, all of which merit an upload onto your Instagram.

Its all affordable too – baked goods and hot drinks are just a couple of quid, and meals between £5 and £7. The minimalist interior is sleekly designed, and comfortable enough to spend an hour or two while you enjoy the great food. It's a rarity to find a veggie café combined with a hairdressers, but somehow The Canary works and is worth a visit.

£
Vegetarian
Some Vegan & Gluten Free

The Gallery Café ❹
HOMEMADE CAFÉ STAPLES
Margaret's House Settlement,
21 Old Ford Road, E2 9PL
www.stmargaretshouse.org.uk
Tel: 020 8980 2092
Open: Mon-Fri 8am-8pm, Sat 9am-8am, Sun 9am-7pm
Unlike many London eateries that try and often fail to keep up with fads and fashions, the Gallery Café is an old-school vegan eatery that can double as either your local or as part of a vegan-friendly day trip, being situated a short stroll from Bethnal Green station and neighbouring the V&A Museum of Childhood.

The food here is ethically sourced, wholesome and unpretentious. Breakfast runs from 8am till 12noon, and the main menu from then until 7pm, 7 days a week. They also have a rotation of seasonal specials, fresh sandwiches and sweet treats, meaning you're unlikely to run out of things to try here. Meals cost £6-£9, drinks between £2 and £4, and their hearty Full English is definitely one to try. The Gallery Café is part of a community based charity, St. Margaret's House – so look out for their yoga classes, charity clothing boutique and cultural events.

£
Vegan

Just FaB 5

VEGAN ITALIAN ON A DOUBLE DECKER BUS

455-459 Hackney Road, E2 9DY
Tel: 0741 4917637
www.just-fab.org
Twitter: @Just_FaB_Vegita
Travel: Bethnal Green LU/ Cambridge Heath LO
Open: Tues-Sun 11.30am-10pm

Just FaB is a vegan Italian eatery that plates up pizzas and pastas in a converted double decker London bus. The upper deck has been converted to hold benches and tables, which can be a bit cramped for groups, but are fine for a casual dinner date with a dash of humour.

Inspired by the owner's roots, you'll find classic Sicilian dishes such as panelle, aranchini and lasagna alongside raw spaghettis. The menu is as fresh as the food, so you can expect specials to keep things surprising. The food isn't gourmet, but the portions are hearty and the prices low, with mains costing around £5, making this a pretty cheap eat. It's worth knowing too that the ingredients are sourced from local suppliers where possible, or from the family-connected farm and food business back in Sicily. The bus's red roof makes the place pretty hard to miss from Hackney Road, so schedule a visit to this fabulous foodie Route Master.

£
Vegan
Some Gluten Free

Sazzy and Fran Café ❻

HOMEMADE CAFÉ STAPLES

17 Gossamer Garden,
The Gossamer City Project, E2 9FN
Tel: 074 2871 7579
Twitter: @sazzyandfran
Insta: @sazzyandfrancafe
Travel: Cambridge Heath LO/Bethnal Green LU
Open: Mon-Sat 8am-5pm

Slotted amongst the Gossamer City Project's container complex, Sazzy and Fran Café is a vegan eatery worth seeking out. Run by the eponymous couple, it serves a range of hearty mains dishes like udon noodle soup and pizza, as well as breakfast bowls and baked treats, all of which rotate on their ever changing menu.

The cooking is simple and wholesome, and you'll be able to find healthy and tasty food whether you're sweet or savoury toothed. Everything is competitively priced, with curries or pancake stacks generally costing as little as £4. There isn't much space at the café however, and you may be confined to al fresco dining, though there are plans to expand into neighbouring containers. Sazzy and Fran Café is a good choice when looking for a quality quick bite in this corner of Hackney, they also offer a take-away service.

£
Vegan
Some Gluten Free

Mildred's Dalston

Dalston

Restaurants, Cafés & Bars:

1) Andu Café
2) Arancini Brothers
3) Fed By Water
4) Gujarati Rasoi
5) Mildred's Dalston
6) Pamela Bar

Shops:

A) Muku Hair, p.350

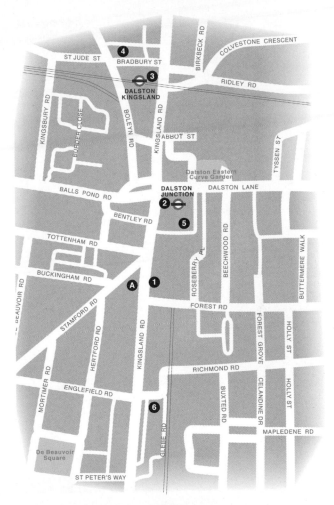

Andu Café ❶

ETHIOPIAN

528 Kingsland Road, E8 4AH
Tel: 020 7254 1780
www.anducafe.co.uk
Travel: Dalston Junction LO
Open: Daily 12noon-10pm

This eatery is a world away from the trend-following vegan spots you would typically associate with Hackney. The only sourdough you'll find here won't come with avocado, but instead as a traditional 'injera' – a spongy flatbread that is perfect for soaking up the rich stews that are typical of Ethiopian cuisine. In fact, Ethiopia is a vegan heartland and is the inspiration behind Rastafarianism's Ital culture.

Andu Café is a good first stop for getting a taste of this healthy cuisine that uses lots of legumes and spinach and enlivens these ingredients with the judicious use of spices. The food comes out as a platter for you to mix and match, which is a great way to sample a range of dishes. The café is a bit of a mishmash itself, with wood cladding and brick effect wall paper, but the effect is homely and the service friendly with advice on hand if needed. Andu Café is a pleasant place for a casual lunch or dinner and you're unlikely to pay more than £7-8 for a comprehensive meal. They are rightly proud of their Ethiopian coffee which is traditionally prepared and a perfect end to a meal here.

£
Vegan

BRANCH

Arancini Brothers ❷

RISOTTO BALLS & FAST FOOD

592 Kingsland Road, E8 4AH
www.arancinibrothers.com, full review see page 69

Fed By Water ❸
ITALIAN
59 Kingsland High Street, E8 2JS
Tel: 020 7249 6242
www.fedbywater.co.uk
Insta: @fedbywater
Travel: Dalston Kingsland LO
Open: Mon-Sun 8am-10pm, Fri-Sat 8am-11pm, Sun 8am-9pm

These days Dalston is home to all things trendy, and Fed By Water is no exception. This eatery is a hot name on the lips of vegans discussing where best to eat in the capital. The selling pitch, other than that they make good Italian food, is that it's all prepared with purified water. We're not sure we're sold by this quirk, but this is still probably the best place in the East End to enjoy a cuisine that is so often reliant on meat and dairy. Attractive pizzas, pastas and 'cheese' platters are the main dishes here, utilising classic recipes but with innovative vegan ingredients like soy ricotta.

Dishes are on the pricier end of the spectrum, with their Margherita being the cheapest option for £9, and most pastas, cheese platters and pizzas being in the mid teens. With soft drinks at £3, beers £6 and wine only available by the bottle, a meal here is likely to set you back £25-£30 a head. Despite this, Fed By Water is always busy and, with a pleasant interior and food that is reliably good, it's not hard to see why booking is advisable. Fed By Water might be a little expensive but for a special vegan treat, it's well worth a visit.

££-£££
Vegan
Some Gluten Free and Raw

Gujarati Rasoi ❹
INDIAN GUJARATI
10c Bradbury Street, N16 8JN
Tel: 020 8616 7914
www.gujaratirasoi.com
Twitter: @GujuratiRasoi
Insta: @gujuratirasoi
Travel: Dalston Kingsland LO
Open: Sun-Mon Closed, Tues-Sat 6pm-10.30pm
This intimate Indian restaurant gives you a real flavour of Gujarati cooking. Unlike many Indian restaurants it's open plan, allowing you see your food prepared. The menu is also a little different from standard Indian veggie fair with a more limited menu of carefully prepared original dishes presented in their own unique way. Slow-cooked vegetable curries are packed with aromatic spices with less commonly used regional fruits like pomegranate and tamarind, and marinated paneer all a feature of the menu. Gujarati Rasoi is inexpensive and largely vegan (it's totally vegetarian), making it a great place for casual dining with friends. If you're going with friends try a variety of dishes from their menu to sample all the flavours they have on offer.

Regardless of whether you want to stick to your plate or share, you'll probably pay between £10 and £15 at most per head for a substantial meal. The interior is a little simpler than you might expect from an Indian restaurant but is perfectly in keeping with this original Indian eatery. We're big fans of what this mother and son duo are doing here. If you can't make it to the restaurant they have a stall every Saturday at Broadway Market selling some of the best samosas in the capital.

££
Vegetarian
Some Gluten Free and Raw
Some Vegan

Mildred's Dalston ❺
INTERNATIONAL
1 Dalston Square, E8 3GU
Tel: 020 8017 1815
Full review see page 56

Pamela Bar ❻
INTERNATIONAL / COCKTAIL BAR
428 Kingsland Road, E8 4AA
Tel: 020 7686 3212
www.pamelabar.com
Travel: Dalston Kingsland LO
Open: Tues-Thu 6pm-12midnight, Fri-Sat 6pm-2am
Pamela hosts a string of popular and successful kitchen residencies, such as with Club Mexicana, Mao Chow and What the Fattoush, meaning that great food dishes can be enjoyed alongside cocktails and other drinks on a night out here. In this trendily designed Dalston spot there are plenty of tables and a copper bar space, from where you can dig into a selection of freshly prepared savoury dishes plus the occasional sweet treat here or there. Dishes are priced between £6 and £10, but are sufficiently portioned to serve as a filling main meal. The menu is subject to change, but will likely always feature tasty street food dishes. Pamela is one of the better value eating and drinking holes in the area; it's well worth a visit and might just become one of your regular haunts.

£-££
Vegan

Forest Gate

Shinde's Pure Veg
SOUTH INDIAN
302 Green Street, E7 8LF
www.shindes.com
Tel: 020 8257 1778
Travel: Upton Park LU
Open: Daily 11am-10pm

Vijay's Chawalla
SOUTH INDIAN
268-270 Green Street, E7 8LF
www.vijayschawalla.co.uk
Tel: 020 8470 3535
Travel: Upton Park LU
Open: Daily 11.30am-9pm

Green Street is home to one of the highest densities of
Bangladeshis, Indians and Pakistanis in the capital. Green
Street restaurants reflect this, serving some of the least
anglicised Indian food in the capital, and you'll be able to find
a few vegetarian eateries here serving gold standard South
Indian fare at affordable prices. If you're visiting then Vijay's
or Shinde's are the ones to try. Dosas and chaats – which are
pancakes and fried potato dishes respectively – are reliable
choices to be enjoyed alongside chutneys, sambars and
sauces. The dining spaces are simple, laid back and pleasant
enough to dine in, but the food itself is some of the most
authentic you'll find in London. If you're looking to be bowled
over by new, different flavours, then opt for a thali, tear up some
naan bread and tuck in.

£
Vegetarian

The Spread Eagle

Hackney South

Restaurants, Cafés & Bars:

1) Black Cat Café
2) The Brook
3) Lele's
4) Mother Works
5) Palm Vaults
6) Rehab
7) Smashing Kitchen
8) The Spread Eagle
9) Temple of Hackney
10) The V Deli

Shops

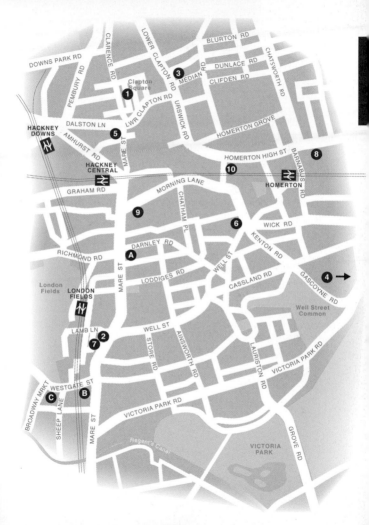

Black Cat Café ❶

CAFÉ STAPLES

76A Clarence Road, E5 8HB
Tel: 020 8985 7091
www.blackcatcafe.co.uk
Insta: @blackcathackney
Travel: Hackney Central LO
Open: Mon, Wed & Thurs 9am-9pm, Fri 9am-10pm,
Sat 11am-10pm, Sun 11am-8pm

Black Cat Café is a great casual vegan eatery; inexpensive, tasty and with extremely generous portions, it makes for a sound alternative to your local greasy spoon in Hackney. Tofish and chips, vegan fry-ups and seitan burgers are the kinds of hearty food you'll find here, served up by friendly volunteers in a casual and comfortable interior.

They've got lighter foods, hot drinks and highly popular milkshakes too. You can easily eat here for around £5, with large mains being only a couple of quid more, and the drinks are also great value. As ethical and cooperative establishments go, Black Cat Café ticks all the boxes. After one visit it's easy to see why Black Cat is among many vegans' favourite places and one well worth seeking out in the back streets of Hackney.

£
Vegan

The Brook ❷
INTERNATIONAL / COCKTAIL BAR
171 Mare Street, E8 3RH
Tel: 020 8617 9470
www.the-brook.co.uk
Insta: @thebrooksocial
Travel: Hackney Central LO/London Fields LO
Open: Wed-Sun 6pm-12midnight

The Brook is a bustling bar and vegan restaurant that's proving popular with Hackney's growing number of cruelty-free residents. The cuisine is varied but focuses largely on international fast food. Menus often feature things like jackfruit burgers and quesadillas, but also French onion soup and meatless Sunday Roasts. Small plates cost between £5 and £7 and mains average between £10 and £14, and cocktails are £8 and £10. At these prices, their sizeably portioned, good-looking food and drinks are competitive with the neighbours. The main eating space is small but trendily decorated, with plenty of neon lights, houseplants and Mexican influences to enjoy.

The drinks list is just as diverse and extensive. Bottles of beer, bubbly and other beverages are all available, but it's the copious cocktail list that is the big draw. The Brook also has a cool subterranean space for events, and offers a catering service too. If the full tables and busy kitchen are anything to go by, The Brook has found its niche and looks destined to be a feature on Hackney's vegan scene for many years to come.

£
Vegan

Lele's ❸
VEGAN PATISSERIE AND CAFÉ

50 Lower Clapton Road, E5 0RN
www.leleslondon.com
Insta: @leles_london
Travel: Hackney Central LU
Open: Mon-Fri 7am-6pm, Sat-Sun 9am-5pm

Clapton has seen a lot of change in recent years, both good and bad, but Lele's is a local café and patisserie that is something to celebrate. Their pastries are edible art pieces in miniature, and they offer popular supper clubs and Sunday afternoon teas alongside their usual brunch service in a small but attractive interior. The menu changes daily, but you can expect salads, soups and sandwiches aplenty and a couple of specials to watch out for, as the chefs are constantly experimenting with new dishes.

The food is light and freshly prepared, completely vegan, and sourced locally where possible. Lele's do some of the best vegan pancakes anywhere, but if you're avoiding gluten there are plenty of available options. Brunch will cost about £10 per person, however, you're not only getting great food, but also supporting a business where you can taste the love that the staff put into the food everyday. Dogs are welcome and there's a friendly rescue pooch in the café called ZZ. Lele's is a great vegan eatery and one that merits a special visit.

£-££
Vegan
Some Gluten Free and Raw

Mother Works ❹
INTERNATIONAL CAFÉ STAPLES
1 Canalside, Here East Estate, E20 3BS
Tel: 0738 8554 060
www.mother.works
Insta: @mother.works
Travel: Hackney Wick LO
Open: Mon-Fri 9am-9pm, Sat-Sun 10am-9pm

Hackney Wick is home to many a hipster happening, and Mother Works is no exception. It's a vegan café and juice maker, providing high quality bottles of fruit and veg juice using local, seasonal and organic produce. Their food is also worth a trip to the canalside running by the Here East estate–they've got great vegan treats like apple and parsnip cake, as well as plant-based savoury dishes such as 'Buddha bowls' and dhals.

If you don't fancy accompanying your meal with a cold-press juice, drinks like Kombucha or Hot Cacao are also on offer. The space is trendily decorated, with plenty of tables, sofas and hanging chairs from which to enjoy your food and relax. The prices aren't too high either, with breakfast, lunch and dinner options like peanut and cauliflower West African curry or Acai bowls costing between £5 and £9. This exclusively vegan eatery is a rarity in the Hackney Wick area and one well worth seeking.

£-££
Vegan
Some Gluten Free and Raw

Palm Vaults ❺

RETRO MIAMI THEMED CAFÉ
411 Mare Street, E8 1HY
www.palmvaults.com
Twitter: @PalmvaultsE8
Insta: @palmvaults
Travel: Hackney Central LO
Open: Mon-Wed 7.30am-6pm, Thu-Fri 7.30am-8pm
Sat 9am-8pm, Sun 9am-5.30pm

Labelled by some as London's most Instagrammable café, Palm Vaults certainly has a remarkable aesthetic, despite being on an unassuming Hackney shopping street. Large potted cheese plants hang from the ceiling above pink marble-top tables, surrounded by bare brick walls. To find all this in the centre of Hackney is no surprise to some, but the niche vibe draws in big crowds and queues to this patch of the East End.

At the weekend the place can get busy when punters come from all over to enjoy a taste of the lavender lattes and vegan chocolate cakes. The food is top notch – it's all vegetarian, with vegan and GF options aplenty, and focuses on brunch café dishes like avocado on toast or light and fruity smoothie bowls & salads, as well as homemade cakes and an array of drinks.

The food is equally photogenic – salads are adorned with flower petals, and smoothie bowls are an experiment in Technicolour. Its worth bearing in mind that you come here strictly for the food, interior and human interaction – there is a no laptops policy. If this is your cup of tea, or if you simply can't get enough of this cool café, they also sell Palm Vaults merchandise.

£-££
Vegetarian
Some Gluten Free
Some Vegan

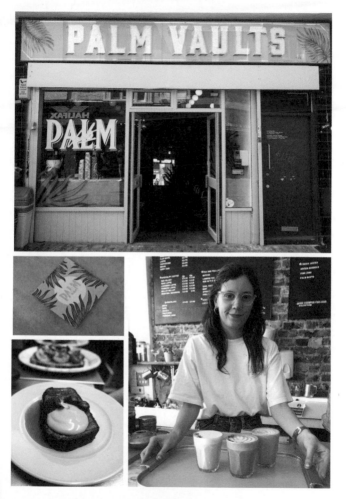

Rehab ❻
INTERNATIONAL
271 Well Street, E9 6RG
Tel: 020 3222 5119
www.rehabhackney.com
Twitter/Insta: @rehabhackney
Travel: Hackney Central LO
Open: Mon-Thurs 10am-4.30pm,
Fri & Sat 10am-9pm (bar till 12pm), Sun 10am-5pm

Rehab is a trendy 'medicinal' vegan café and bar that serves 'healing' foods from its Hackney premises. Alongside sandwiches and salad bowls, it offers a seasonally rotating mains menu and a drinks list that includes spiced lattes, fruity smoothies, craft beers and cocktails.

The Rehab team pride themselves on using local providers and organic produce to make delicious and nutritious vegan dishes. The space itself is beautifully designed in a boho chic manner, with Persian rugs, lush plants against brick walls, and a perfect balance between natural and artificial lighting. It all makes for a setting that offers a welcome escape from this run-down end of Well Street. The prices are higher than average for this part of the capital, but competitive with other organic-only establishments. Mains and brunches cost between £7 for sandwiches and £14 for salad bowls, but these are all good value considering how sizeable and packed with diverse ingredients they are. Rehab also runs events here for the local community, which range from parent nights to art exhibitions and yoga and meditation classes. Rehab is definitely worth a try if you're in this corner of Hackney and a great place to relax and watch the world go by from its extensive glass fronted façade.

££
Vegan
Some Gluten Free and Raw

Smashing Kitchen ❼
INTERNATIONAL
1a Bayford Street, E8 3SE
Tel: 020 8525 1118
www.smashingkitchen.co.uk
Insta: @smashingkitchen
Travel: Hackney Central LO/London Fields LO
Open: Mon-Thurs 8.30am-4.30pm and 5.30pm-9pm,
Fri 8.30am-4.30pm and 5.30pm-10pm, Sat 9am-5pm

This bright, clean eatery is a welcome addition to London's vegan scene. The décor is all pale wood, houseplants and cacti, with a white tiled floor giving the place a spacious feel. The owner, Asia, only started the business in the spring of 2018 and is always on-hand to make sure her customers are relaxed and enjoying a vegan menu that offers a range of fresh salads, homemade falafels and wraps. The portions are generous and there's also a changing specials' board showcasing seasonal produce.

   If you don't fancy a full vegan blowout they thoughtfully offer a range of light snacks and sharing plates, so customers can sit and graze without breaking the bank. The food is lovingly prepared and the butter bean humous makes a tasty change from the usual chickpea staple. Although only just finding its feet, Smashing Kitchen already has a loyal following among the workers and locals of this Hackney enclave. Smashing Kitchen are big dog lovers and your pooch is guaranteed a warm welcome after a stroll on nearby London Fields.

£
Vegan
Some Gluten Free and Raw

The Spread Eagle ❽
VEGAN PUB AND MEXICAN FOOD
224 Homerton High Street, E9 6AS
Tel: 020 8985 0400
www.thespreadeaglelondon.co.uk
Twitter: @SpreadEagleLDN
Insta: @thespreadeaglelondon
Travel: Homerton LU
Open: Mon-Thurs 4pm-11pm, Fri 4pm-2am,
Sat 12noon-2am, Sun 12noon-11pm

Six years after Soho saw the first veggie pub open in the capital at Norman's (see p.59), Hackney has welcomed London's first vegan pub with open arms.

This strictly plant-based establishment has taken Club Mexicana under its wing to serve up great Mexican street food here, as well as a list of 16 animal product free beers and ales on tap that are really worth trying. Expect meatless scallops and chicken wings, tortas, tacos and tortillas. Snacks and sides cost between £4 and £6, and bigger meals between £7 and £10. If a Beavertown and burrito doesn't match up to your idea of a pub, you needn't worry. The regulars who have been coming for years are equally welcome as the new crowd, ensuring that you still get a proper pub vibe, despite the polished and trendy interior. The place is family and dog friendly during the day, and hosts lively music nights and slightly wilder events like drag shows in the evenings. If this isn't a testament to how veganism can be for everyone then we don't know what is – whether you're teetotal or drinker, this is a must-visit for a vegan good time in east London.

£-££
Vegan

Temple of Hackney ❾
VEGAN FRIED CHICKEN
10 Morning Lane, E9 6NA
www.templeofseitan.co.uk
Insta: @templeofseitan
Travel: Hackney Central LO
Open: Mon-Sat 12noon-9pm, Sun 12noon-6pm

Temple of Seitan hardly need introducing. They took the chicken shop – Britain's most popular street food – and transformed it into a delicious vegan treat. As pioneers of vegan street food they enjoyed instant success with long queues for their deep fried seitan. The hype might have died down, but their following has remained strong and further branches have followed.

Seitan, or wheat meat, might sound a bit glutinous for your liking, but the Temple's faux chicken isn't far off the real deal you'd get from KFC. The batter balances crunch against the bite of the 'chicken', creating a texture that's difficult to differentiate from meat. The spicy burger and wrap are equally good here, but the wings with buffalo sauce can be a bit hit and miss. The menu features decent chips, slaw and mac'n'cheese too – allowing you to enjoy a substantial and filling meal. The prices are very reasonable – £6 gets you a great burger and just add £2 for chips and a drink. The Hackney outlet is laid out like a glossy chicken shop but unfortunately lacks indoor seating, and the couple of outdoor benches ironically face the neighbouring halal butchers. Regardless, there's no excuse not to ditch your Dixy's and try one of the capital's most popular vegan indulgences.

Branches:
Temple of Camden, 103a Camley Street, N1C 4PF, See page 284
Temple of Goods, Hackney Downs Studios, 17 Amhurst Terrace, E8 2BT, See page 138

£
Vegan & Some Gluten Free

The V Deli ⑩

CAFÉ STAPLES

215 Ponsford Street, E9 6JU
www.vdelicious.co.uk
Twitter/Insta: @vdeliciouscake
Travel: Homerton LO
Open: Mon-Thurs 9am-6pm, Fri 9am-2pm, Sun 10am-6pm

The V Deli is a small eatery under some railway arches that sells a range of vegan goods to be enjoyed at a couple of tables and chairs in-store, or can be taken away or ordered via UberEats. They sell organic juices and hot drinks, wraps, salads and burgers, tarts, pastries and other baked goods. The vegan pastries are freshly made and delicious and aren't too expensive either, costing between £1.50 and £3. However, their main meals are on the pricey side, costing between £12.50 and £14.50, and juices are close to the £5 mark. It's always good to see new cruelty-free businesses though and their vegan pastries are definitely worth a try.

££
Vegan

CookDaily

Spitalfields, Shoreditch & Brick Lane

Restaurants, Cafés & Bars:

1) The Canvas Café and Creative Space
2) CookDaily
3) Crosstown Doughnuts
4) Dark Sugars Chocolates
5) Dark Sugars Cocoa House
6) Essence Cuisine
7) Essential Vegan Café
8) Mooshies
9) Pilpel Old Spitalfields Market
10) Pilpel Spitalfields (Brushfield)
11) Plates
12) Redemption
13) Unripe Banana
14) Vegan Yes
15) Veggie Pret
16) Vida Vegan Bakery
17) The Vurger Co
18) What the Pitta

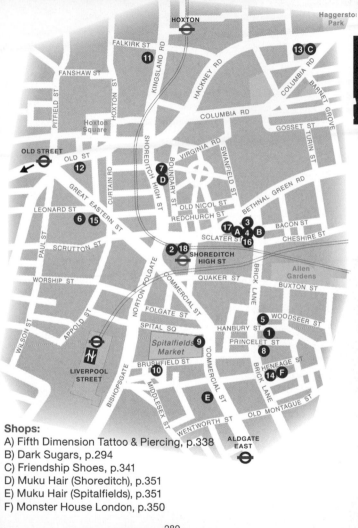

Shops:
A) Fifth Dimension Tattoo & Piercing, p.338
B) Dark Sugars, p.294
C) Friendship Shoes, p.341
D) Muku Hair (Shoreditch), p.351
E) Muku Hair (Spitalfields), p.351
F) Monster House London, p.350

The Canvas Café and Creative Space ❶

HOMEMADE CAFÉ STAPLES
42 Hanbury Street, E1 5JL
Tel: 020 7018 1020
www.thecanvascafe.org
Twitter: @TheCanvasCafe
Insta: @thecanvascafee1
Travel: Liverpool Street LU/LO/Rail
Open: Mon-Tues 11am-8pm, Wed-Thu 11am-10pm,
Fri 11am-12midnight, Sat-Sun 10am-8pm

The Canvas Café and Creative Space is something a little unusual for Shoreditch. It's a vegan eatery that serves homemade breakfasts and lunches throughout much of the day, as well as delicious desserts.

You can expect to find hearty Tofish and Chips, a vegan Full English or a substantial freakshake and if you fancy something stronger, they also sell alcoholic drinks. They do some mock meat sandwiches too, which are best enjoyed with a bowl of chips for those with a large appetite. Breakfasts cost between £6 and £9, lunches are £10-£11, and sweet things less, making the Canvas Café price competitive for the area considering its wares are all homemade.

Their subterranean creative space plays host to regular live performances, film nights and other free events like yoga and mindfulness, as part of their community outreach mission. They're also a step or two away from Second Home and the Liberia bookshop, which are two top London enterprises that are well worth a visit.

£-££
Vegan

CookDaily ❷

INTERNATIONAL
BoxPark Shoreditch E1 6GY
www.cookdaily.co.uk
Twitter/Insta: @kingcookdaily
Tel: 074 9856 3168
Travel: Shoreditch High Street LO
Open: Mon-Wed 12noon-9pm, Thurs-Sat 12noon-10:30pm,
Sun 12noon-12midnight

Situated within the ever-trendy BoxPark, CookDaily rightly feels like the 'king' of plant-based street food. The owner King Cook channels his Laotian heritage when firing out bowls of South-East Asian goodness, which are remarkably popular with the crowds milling around the BoxPark. The eatery aims to promote veganism as a lifestyle for all with its photogenic meat-free Pad Thai, curries and quirkier dishes like hemp-based Full English's. Between visits you might find additions to the menu, and their spring rolls are among the most popular items available – perfect as a quick snack or accompaniment to a meal.

CookDaily bowls cost £9 and smoothies for £4, which given the ingredients and location is reasonable. You can expect to start enjoying your food within 5 to 10 minutes of ordering, but be mindful of queues and limited seating during peak service hours. The ethos driving CookDaily is hard to rival, and it really is a must visit among the numerous vegan outlets in Shoreditch.

£-££
Vegan

Crosstown Shoreditch ❸

157 Brick Lane, E1 6SB
www.crosstowndoughnuts.com
Tel: 020 7729 3417
Full review see page 46

CookDaily

Dark Sugars
CHOCOLATIER

Dark Sugars Chocolates, 141 Brick Lane, E1 6SB **4**
Tel: 07429 472 606
•Chocolate Shop

Dark Sugars Cocoa House, 124-126 Brick Lane, E1 6RU **5**
Tel: 07429 472 606
•Chocolate Café

www.darksugars.co.uk
Twitter: @DarkSugars
Insta: @darksugars
Travel: Shoreditch High Street LO/Liverpool Street LU
Open: Daily 10am-10pm
Shoreditch has seen its fair share of niche restaurants and shops
come and go. Dark Sugars, however, have not only kept their doors
firmly open, but, a testament to the quality of their produce and its
popularity, have opened a second branch just down the road. Both
outlets boast a ridiculous variety of both vegan and dairy-based
chocolate truffles. We can't get enough of their vegan stem ginger
chocolates, but whether it's popping candy, sea-salt caramel
pearls or chocolate & rum liqueurs that you're after, just follow the
sweet scent of cocoa on any visit to Brick Lane. Prices are based
on weight in-store or fixed rates for online sales, but the quality of
these handcrafted chocolates is worth every penny. Particularly
recommended for the perfect gift, not least for their immaculate
presentation, are Dark Sugars' 'signature boxes'.

££
Vegetarian
Vegan
Gluten Free

Essence Cuisine ⑥
VEGAN, GLUTEN-FREE AND RAW CAFÉ
94 Leonard Street, EC2A 4RH
Tel: 020 7729 5678
www.essence-cuisine.com
Insta: @essence_cuisine
Travel: Old Street LU/Shoreditch High Street LO
Open: Mon 8am-7pm, Tue-Fri 8am-9pm,
Sat 9am-9pm, Sun 9am-7pm

Behind an unassuming exterior on Leonard Street you'll find an aluminium-walled cuboid, with ultra-modern concrete, metal and wooden surfaces, which proves the perfect backdrop to Essence Cuisine's artful menu.

Avocado on toast and vegan cheese platters appear as if from a contemporary art gallery. Attractive salad bowls and sushi rolls feature alongside pizzas, pastas and puddings, which are all free from animal products, gluten and refined sugars, and often prepared raw. Celebrity chef Matthew Kenney, has put healthy eating and fresh ingredients at the heart of his menu and the dishes that emerge from the state-of-the-art kitchen are as delicious as they are beautiful.

Organic produce and local providers are used wherever possible, as well as quirkier ingredients like dragonfruit and fermented coconut. Despite all this, prices are reasonable with brunches and puddings for £7, and main meals for £7-£14. They also offer Essence Express – a takeout service that is available in-store and from the delivery services UberEats and Deliveroo. Essence Cuisine is an experience, and a great place to try vegan and raw food at its best.

£-££
Vegan
Gluten Free
Raw

Essential Vegan Café ❼

BRAZILIAN

6 Calvert Avenue, E2 7JP

Tel: 020 7739 3628

www.essentialvegan.uk

Twitter/Insta: @essentialvegan

Travel: Old Street LU/Shoreditch High Street LO

Open: Tues-Fri 12noon-9pm, Sat 11am-9pm,
Sun 11am-7pm

This treat of a Shoreditch eatery is a Brazilian café that specialises in making meaty vegan burgers. It also offers hard-to-source regional fare, which is inspired by the chef-owner's Brazilian heritage, with dishes like Coxinha and Moqueca casserole featured on the menu. You needn't worry about the association with animal products that Brazilian cuisine so often has, as here they've replaced these with great substitutes like seitan and jackfruit.

Lighter options include salad and quiche and there are plenty of sweet treats like passion fruit cheesecake. The food is reasonably priced and with an open kitchen you can be sure your dish is freshly made to order. The space is small but cosy in its simplicity, with wooden tables and a changing display of local artwork adorning the walls. Located in one of Shoreditch's quieter back streets, Essential Vegan Café is a great place to relax, enjoy good food and escape the crowds of nearby Brick Lane and Shoreditch High Street.

£

Vegan

Some Gluten Free

Mooshies ❽
BURGER BAR
104 Brick Lane, E1 6RL
Tel: 07931 842458
www.veganburger.org
Insta: @mooshieslondon
Travel: Liverpool Street LU/Shoreditch High Street LO
Open: Tues-Sun 12noon till late

Shoreditch is the bastion of East London's plant-based eating scene, and its main artery – Brick Lane – has a host of restaurants and shops to meet this demand. Mooshies is among the best. Nestled on a corner half way down the road, it offers vegan burgers that are some of the meatiest and yet meat-free you'll find in the capital – a must-try for carnivores curious about ethical food choices. Bean burgers are infamously bland in most eateries, but Mooshies' 'WHAT'S YOUR BEEF?' classic is sure to raise some pulses, and their pulled jackfruit and 'phish' options have mastered the art of culinary deception –check out their Instagram for tempting images. Considering the location and ingredients used, their tempting burgers are great value. Mooshies is a popular place but there is plenty of seating and the service is fast, making this a great place to visit if your in search of good value vegan fast food.

£
Vegan

BRANCH

Pilpel ❾
Old Spitalfields Market,
Unit E, Pavillion Building, E1 6EW
Tel: 020 7375 2282
www.www.pilpel.co.uk
Full review see page 24

Mooshies

BRANCH

Pilpel ⑩
Spitalfields (Brushfield)
38 Brushfield Street, E1 6AT
Tel: 0207 952 5768
www.www.pilpel.co.uk
Full review see page 24

Plates ⑪
INTERNATIONAL FINE DINING
93 Kingsland Road, Hoxton, E2 8AG
www.plates-london.com
Instagram/Twitter: @plates_london
Travel: Hoxton LO/Old Street LU
Open: Sats only, tickets to be booked in advance, see website

Plates cook the most eccentric vegan food in the capital. They're an experimental dining company formed by a brother and sister duo with experience working in some of the most respected kitchens and design studios around, including the renowned three-starred French Laundry. Plates is only open to the public on Saturdays, and you should book well in advance, but it really is worth the wait. A £40 ticket allows you to enjoy a 5-course, seasonal menu that experiments with only the best organic or wild fruits and vegetables. With their tarts, curries, broths and much more, Plates demonstrate that there is no limit to meat-free, dairy-free and sugar-free cuisine. Their Instagram attests to this, where you'll see dishes like shiitake and celeriac lasagne composed as if they're an edible sculpture.

Plates also has a drinks menu, both alcoholic and non-alcoholic, that curates some of the best speciality teas, house-made cocktails, and natural wines available. The dining experience here is enhanced by the beautiful interior, which features sleek Scandinavian minimalist furnishing, stripped back lighting and tasteful art pieces. Plates might not be the easiest place to visit, but the effort and wait is well worth it. It's one of the best places in London to visit for a vegan special occasion.

£££££
Vegan
Some Gluten Free and Raw

Branch

Redemption 🔟

VEGAN, GLUTEN-FREE AND RAW CAFÉ
320 Old Street, EC1V 9DR
Tel: 020 7613 0720
www.redemptionbar.co.uk
Full review see page 165

Unripe Banana 🔢

CAFÉ STAPLES
Unit 7, 268 Hackney Road, E2 7SJ
www.unripebanana.co.uk
Insta: @unripebanana
Travel: Cambridge Heath LO
Open: Tues-Fri 8am-4pm, Sat-Sun 10am-5pm

Unripe Banana is a trendy multi-purpose space that has a vegan café and clothes shop upstairs, and a gallery space downstairs displaying work for sale by local artists. Food and drink-wise, they've got plenty of artisan coffees, teas, spiced lattes and mylks. In terms of food they offer a reasonable selection of sandwiches, brownies or pastries.

The food is reliably good and the prices low, making this a good food stop if you're in the area. Their retail stock is mostly Lucy and Yak dungarees, and they only sell ethical brand goods. The space is small, with only a couple of tables and chairs, but Unripe Banana also offers a take away service if you don't mind eating on the go.

£
Vegan

Vegan Yes ⑭
ITALIAN KOREAN FUSION
64 Brick Lane, E1 6RF
Tel: 0787 9536 269
www.veganyes.uk
Insta: @vegan_yes
Travel: Shoreditch High Street LO/ Liverpool Street LU
Open: Daily 11.30am-9pm
Not the usual vegan fare, but one that works all the same – Vegan Yes serves an Italian and Korean fusion cuisine from its two branches in north and east London. Food ranges from pasta dishes like lasagne, gnocchi and zuppa, to Korean wraps, salads and sushi-like dishes called gimbap, most of which are loaded up with kimchi. The majority of the dishes are a mix of the two cuisines which makes for an interesting culinary experience. They also serve a good choice of drinks, both alcoholic and not, as well as a couple of dessert dishes like chocolate-coated rice balls called mochi. Their street food offering is expensive, even if it is homemade, with 'large' pasta dishes costing between £10 and £15. Their Nag's Head Market space is a hole-in-the-wall operation, offering an exclusively takeaway menu, but their Shoreditch eatery has a few chairs and tables allowing you to eat in. Vegan Yes's Korean cum Italian food is an unusual fusion, but one worth a try.

Branch: 22 Seven Sisters Road, Nag's Head Market, N7 6AG
For review see page 111

££
Vegan

BRANCH

Veggie Pret ⑮
VEGGIE ONLY SANDWICH SHOP
www.pret.co.uk
57 Great Eastern Street, EC2A 3QD
Full review see page 60

Vida Vegan Bakery ⑯
BAKERY AND CAFÉ
139 Brick Lane, E1 6SB
Twitter: @vidabakery
Insta: @vidabakery
Open: Thurs 10am-8pm, Fri 10am-8pm, Sat 11am-8pm,
Sun 11am-6pm, Mon 12noon-7pm, Tues-Wed 10am-7pm
Vane and Dani have been providing delicious vegan sweet
treats at markets and events for a while, but their cute little
shop only arrived on Brick Lane in the summer of 2018. Having
a place of their own has brought out Vida's aesthetic instincts
with a smart moss-green shop front and clean white interior,
made more welcoming with comfy cushioned benches and a
changing display of artwork.

The cupcakes come in a range of flavours including Oreo,
double chocolate and lemon cheesecake, and are all freshly
baked and taste as delicious as they look. If the display of
cupcakes doesn't take your fancy they also have a choice of
cakes, brownies and cookies from which to choose including
their signature Rainbow Cake. Vida also serves great coffee
and soft drinks to accompany your guilt-free, sweet treat.
Brick Lane can get a little hectic at times and Vida offers a
welcome calm space in which to relax and watch the world go
by beyond its large glass shop front. Dani and Vane have not
entirely settled down and still find time to set up at occasional
vegan markets and events like Vegan Nights and also make
and bake vegan cakes to order – three-tiered Oreo wedding
cake anyone?

£
Vegan
Gluten Free

The Vurger Co 🔞

BURGER BAR

9 Avant Garde Richmix Square, Cygnet Street, E1 6LD
Tel: 020 3222 0049
www.thevurgerco.com
Twitter/Insta: @thevurgerco
Travel: Shoreditch High Street LO/Liverpool Street LU
Open: Sun-Thurs 12noon-10pm, Fri-Sat 12noon-10.30pm

This on-trend burger joint is doing everything right as far as vegan eating goes. It's located among Rich Mix's cultural complex, which includes a popular cinema and events space and is just a few minutes stroll from Brick Lane. The Vurger Co is tackling the meat industry where it hurts – fast food – by making healthy, plant-based patties that really hit the spot. Rather than relying on the ubiquitous seitan or faux meats, they've opted to go veggie-rich, utilising peppers, aubergines and mushrooms, as well as plenty of pulses, wedged between classic condiments and butter-free brioche buns. Their fries, shakes and desserts are also well worth a try, as is their unctuous mac'n'cheese and they also offer craft beer by the bottle.

Though the grub here is great for an on-the-go bite, there are plenty of seats inside, set among a tasteful modern interior. The prices are competitive, with burgers costing £8.50, and sides, sweet treats and drinks costing between £3 and £5. It's all thumbs up for the Vurger Co, but just remember to bring your plastic, as they don't take cash.

£-££
Vegan
Some Gluten Free

The Vurger Co

Branch

What the Pitta! 18
VEGAN KEBAB
Boxpark Shoreditch, Unit 52
www.whatthepitta.com
Full review see page 93

Walthamstow

Hornbeam Café & Environmental Centre
COMMUNITY CAFÉ WITH LOCAL ORGANIC FOCUS

458 Hoe Street, E17 9AH
Tel: 020 8558 6880
www.hornbeam.org.uk/café
Travel: Leyton Midland Road LO/ Walthamstow Central LU
Open: Wed-Sun 10am-5pm

You're a little spoilt for choice with veggie cafés in east London, but Hornbeam is more than that. A community focused institution, it goes beyond just serving food, hosting daily events and initiatives, from yoga and cycling trips to film nights and workshops that are open to all.

The food itself is served from Wednesday to Sunday and is organic, with fruits and veg almost entirely sourced from local allotments and small-scale organic farmers and the bread is baked in house. The food prepared here is very much as you'd expect from a vegan café with 'fry ups', salads, soups and quiches all on the menu and a variety of dishes that come and go depending on the season. The difference here is that the meals are freshly made and always delicious and the prices are incredibly low with a substantial meal costing around the £6 mark and an all-day vegan brunch, with organic juice and tea or coffee for just £10. The Hornbeam is a gem with a loyal following among the locals and one well worth going out of your way to visit.

£
Vegan

Hornbeam Café & Environmental Centre

Branch

Bodega 50
HOMEMADE CAFÉ STAPLES
442 Hoe Street, E17 9AH
Insta: @bodega50
Full review see page 130

Bühler + Co

VEGGIE AND VEGAN CAFÉ USING LOCAL PRODUCERS

8 Chingford Road, E17 4PJ
Tel: 020 8527 3652
www.buhlerandco.com
Insta: @buhler_and_co
Travel: Walthamstow Central LU
Open: Mon-Wed 8am-5pm, Thur-Fri 8am-10.30pm,
Sat 9am-10.30pm, Sun 9am-5pm

The residents of Walthamstow are lucky to have such a good café tucked away within their suburban sprawl. In the light-filled and minimal interior, Bühler + Co serve vegetarian and vegan café staples but with gourmet ingredients and presentation. Their French toast is a real treat, they make a mean veggie fry-up and do a range of quirky cakes including unusual ingredients like quinoa. They also offer dinner service on certain evenings, featuring creative bowls inspired by Asian cuisine, with our favourites being laksa, dumplings with plum sauce and the especially aesthetic bao buns.

The prices are a bit more than you'd usually expect to pay in the area, with substantial dishes costing at least £8, but then again this isn't any old café. They also source a lot of their produce from some of the best regional suppliers, like Climpson and Sons for their coffee and Chegworth Valley juices. Bühler + Co hosts regular events in their large space (which extends into the back and garden), including exhibitions by local artists. Walthamstow might be a distance for many to travel, but Bühler + Co is well worth seeking out.

££
Vegetarian

Whitechapel

Ten Cable Street
VEGAN DINNER AND EVENT SPACE
10 Cable Street, E1 8JG
Tel: 020 7702 4533
www.tencablestreet.com
Twitter/Insta: @tencablestreet
Travel: Aldgate East LU
Open for pre-booked events only

Based within a former pub, (incidentally the first public house in the capital to ban racial segregation), Ten Cable Street is an events space that helps to promote better living. In collaboration with other vegan and ethical brands and businesses, it hosts supper clubs with menus featuring diverse dishes like dim sum, ribs or cheese and wine. If you want to improve your home cooking they also run workshops as well as talks on how you can incorporate veganism and ethical practices into your own life. For those who want to try things beyond the dinner table, they also offer classes in parenting, meditation and yoga.

Ten Cable Street is not only a great space to learn, but it also acts as a community hub where you can meet like-minded people interested in learning. The space is all sleek wooden floors, brick walls and minimalist light fittings and furniture, making it equally suited to ambient yoga classes and lively dinners. If you're looking for a vegan community to be part of, or just for a one-off dinner with a difference, check out Ten Cable Street's website to see their current programme.

Branch

Pilpel
FALAFELS
60 Alie Street, E1 8PX
www.pilpel.co.uk
Full review see page 24

OUTSKIRTS

Chingford

Feel Good Café
CAFÉ STAPLES
49 Station Road, E4 7DA
Tel: 0779 996 5611
www.thefeelgoodcafe.com
Twitter: @TheFeelGoodFood
Insta: @thefeelgoodfood
Travel: Chingford Rail
Open: Mon-Sat 10am-3pm

The Feel Good Café is a small vegan eatery inside the village arcade that serves healthy breakfasts and lunches during the week in an area with few meat-free options. Porridge and pancakes, topped with oodles of fruit, can be enjoyed with colourful smoothies or coffees; their bean-filled stews are also popular.

They're a fairly prominent CBD oil producer, which can be bought from their website. Considering the area and what you're getting, prices are fairly expensive, with smoothies costing £5 and beans and mushrooms on toast for £8.50. You can however volunteer at Feel Good Café's local allotment (where they grow some produce) in exchange for free meals and drinks. The place doesn't have much seating, but the food is still some of the best in the area, especially for vegans and vegetarians. You can order their food via UberEats.

£-££
Vegan
Some Gluten Free and Raw

Ealing

Vegan HQ
FAST FOOD AND SHOP GOODS
50 St Mary's Street, W5 5EU
www.veganhq.co.uk
Twitter/Insta:@veganhquk
020 8579 4717
Travel: Ealing Broadway LU
Open: Tues-Fri 11am-5.30pm, Sat 10am-5.30pm,
Sun 10.30am-4.30pm

Vegan HQ is a small vegan café and mini market that stocks a selection of vegan products, and also serves hot fast foods, like burgers, kebabs and pasta, as well as cakes and coffee. The grub isn't gourmet, but tasty, filling and affordable food is guaranteed. Prices range between £4 and £7.50 for hot meals, and a couple of quid for drinks and snacks. There is a limited amount of indoor and outdoor seating available at Vegan HQ, but the food is equally well suited to being eaten as a takeaway. Vegan HQ really shines as a source for hard-to-find vegan products like faux meats and cheeses, making this place a really valuable resource for locals.

£
Vegan

Feltham

Super Singh's
FAST FOOD WITH INDIAN TWIST
142 Faggs Road, Feltham, TW14 0NB
Tel: 020 8384 3132
www.supersinghs.co.uk
Twitter: @Supersinghs
Travel: Hatton Cross LU
Open: Mon-Thurs & Sun 12noon-10pm,
Fri 12noon-11pm, Sat 2pm-11pm

Super Singh's is a fast food joint providing Hounslow with all the humour and vegetarian grub they might need. The first thing you'll notice about the place is its colourful façade, adorned with a turban-wearing Sikh Superman, and you'll find the inside to be a similarly light-hearted celebration of the owners' faith.

This is a fitting interior within which to enjoy casual yet colourful meat-free food that ranges from vegan pizzas to spicy paneer and faux fish fillet burgers. There are plenty of sides, smoothies and Indian soft drinks to be enjoyed alongside the food. Everything is competitively priced – you can expect to leave fit to burst for between £5 and £10 a head. They also operate as a takeout, and you can order their food via JustEat. It might be a bit out of the way for most, but if you're in the area Super Singh's is well worth a visit.

£
Vegetarian

Harrow

Ahimsa Café
INTERNATIONAL
7 Red Lion Parade, HA5 3JD
Tel: 020 7018 2133
www.thevegancafe.com
Insta: @ahimsathevegancafepinner
Travel: Pinner LU
Open: Mon 10am-4pm, Tues-Thurs 10am-5.30pm,
Fri-Sat 10am-9.30pm, Sun 10am-8.30pm

Perhaps a bit too far out for most, but Ahimsa Café is a top option for any vegans in Harrow looking for a good meal. This plant-based eatery serves hot breakfasts and lunches throughout the week, and also runs a dinner service on the weekends. Their breakfasts include coconut and chia seed porridge and 'Full English's'. Lunch is mostly wraps and salad bowls and dinner has some more indulgent options like pizza and mac'n 'cheese. For those looking for just a snack, there are both sweet and savoury options, as well as juices, smoothies and hot beverages. Ahimsa is good value, with most things costing between £4 and £6. It's a great café and the only dedicated vegan eatery in the area.

£
Vegan

Branch

Sagar
SOUTH INDIAN
57 Station Road, North Harrow, HA2 7SR
Tel: 020 8861 5757
www.sagarveg.co.uk
Full review see page 40

Kingston

Riverside Vegetaria
INTERNATIONAL
64 High Street,
Kingston upon Thames, KT1 1HN
Tel: 020 8546 7992
www.riversidevegetaria.co.uk
Travel: Norbiton/ Hampton Wick Rail
Open: Mon-Sat 12noon-11pm, Sun 12noon-10pm

This award-winning vegetarian eatery in Kingston takes a no-fuss approach to food without compromising on quality, and is a great option for Kingston's meat-free diners. It serves big portions of a menu that takes its inspiration from across the world, with Caribbean casseroles featuring next to kedgeree, curry and lasagne.

Nearly all of the food is vegan and uses fresh, organic ingredients. They also have an impressive range of vegan drinks, ranging from wines and spirits to soft drinks and hot beverages. The space is simple, yet pleasantly decorated, with the main attraction being the 'French window' view onto the Thames, which doubles into a great al fresco dining space when the weather allows. It's priced competitively for the area, with starters for £7 and mains for £10. It's not gourmet food, but is hearty, healthy and well worth a visit if you're visiting Kingston.

£-££
Vegetarian
Vegan options

Wembley

Sakonis
ASIAN
127-129 Ealing Road, Wembley,
Middlesex, HA0 4BP
Tel: 020 8903 9601
www.sakonis.co.uk
Twitter: @sakonis
Insta: @sakonis_uk
Travel: Alperton LU
Open: Mon-Fri 12noon-9.30pm, Sat-Sun 9am-11am & 12noon-10pm

Sakonis has two restaurants in West London serving a mix-and-match of foods, largely focusing on Indian street food like bhel poori but also featuring Chinese dishes, chips and pizza. They serve small and big plates of dosas and daals, and plenty of accompanying curries, with the large majority of these being both vegan and gluten free.

Though Sakonis operates as a self-service buffet, they have fixed prices, with most plates costing between £4 and £8 each. The interiors are plain but comfortable, and there's enough seating for booking to be unnecessary and they also run a take away service. In short, Sakonis offer good, no frills largely Indian fare, to anyone looking for a cheap vegetarian eatery in the area.

> Branch:
> 330 Uxbridge Road, Pinner, HA5 4HR

£
Vegetarian

Friendship Shoes

Shops
& Services

Central

Alara Health Store
VEGETARIAN FOOD STORE AND DELI
58 Marchmont Street, WC1N 1AB
Tel: 020 7837 1172
www.alarashop.com
Travel: King's Cross LU
Open: Mon-Fri 9am-7pm, Sat 10am-7pm, Sun 11am-6pm
One of the first eateries to cater for vegetarians in central
London, Alara now survives amid a plethora of vegan and
veggie restaurants around King's Cross. Functioning primarily
as a vegetarian health foods store, it stocks a range of products
like herbal remedies, pre-packaged sandwiches and dairy-free
milks. They also have a pay-by-weight buffet service selling
dishes such as stuffed aubergines and leafy salads, which
are popular with both regulars and passersby. Bear in mind,
however, if buying food from here you are limited to sitting
outdoors or taking your food away.

The store offers an extensive and carefully chosen range
including Ren and Green People skincare and a choice of
cruelty-free cosmetics from the likes of Dr.Hauschka as well as
a good selection of groceries. Alara has a great atmosphere,
reasonably priced groceries and health food products and is a
good choice for a buffet meal on fine days.

££
Vegetarian

Neal's Yard Remedies

15 Neal's Yard, WC2H 9DP
Tel: 020 7379 7222
www.nealsyardremedies.com
Twitter:@NYR_Official
Insta: @nyr_official
Travel: Covent Garden LU
Open: Mon-Sat 10am-8pm, Sun 11am-6.30pm

Neal's Yard Remedies is a household name, and for good reason. It has been producing natural organic health and beauty products for decades, ranging from skincare to aromatherapy to supplements. They even stock diffusers and books on healing foods and remedies. All their products are certified Cruelty Free and recognised by major ethical trade markers like Fairtrade and PETA. Their shops also offer therapy rooms and courses covering acupuncture, nutritional workshops and more. Neal's Yard Remedies is a unique independent store and one that should be firmly in the minds of health-conscious vegans.

Planet Organic

23-24 Tottenham Court Road, W1T 1BJ
Tel: 020 3073 1038
www.planetorganic.com
Twitter/Insta: @planetorganicuk
Travel: Tottenham Court Road LU
Open: Mon-Fri 7.30am-9pm, Sat 8am-9pm, Sun 12noon-6pm

London's largest organic supermarket chain has been in business for over 20 years and there's not much that Planet Organic can't do for you. As well as selling their own brand produce, they offer a wealth of goods from various providers that includes food supplements, fresh groceries, eco-cleaning and cruelty-free beauty products. They've even ventured into sustainable furniture, with their Planet Organic Living line. When using their online shop you can tailor your product searches to specific dietary requirements, such as vegan, gluten free and raw. Their stores offer salad bars and other food-to-go, as well as juices and coffee, in case you need a bite to eat while doing the weekly shop. If you have your own containers, some stores now offer plastic-free dispensaries for everyday goods like nuts and grains. Meat and dairy is sold here, but the growing emphasis is towards free-from products. Delivery is available throughout the UK.

BRANCHES:

WANDSWORTH 52 Garratt Lane, SW18 4FT
Tel: 020 8877 8330; Travel: East Putney LU
Open: Mon-Sat 7.30am-9pm, Sunday 9am-9pm

WESTBOURNE GROVE 42 Westbourne Grove, W2 5SH
Tel: 020 7727 2227; Travel: Royal Oak/Bayswater LU
Open: Mon-Sat 7.30am-9.30pm, Sun 12noon-6pm

DEVONSHIRE SQUARE 10 Devonshire Square, EC2M 4AE
Tel: 020 7220 9060; Travel: Liverpool Street LU
Open: Mon-Fri 7.30am-9pm

TORRINGTON PLACE 22 Torrington Place WC1E 7HJ
Tel: 020 7436 1929; Travel: Goodge Street
Open: Mon-Fri 7.30am-9pm, Sat 8am-8pm, Sun 12noon-6pm

ISLINGTON 64 Essex Road, N1 8LR
Tel: 020 7288 9460, Travel: Angel LU
Open: Mon-Sat 7.30am-9.30pm, Sun 9am-9pm

MUSWELL HILL 111-117 Muswell Hill Road, N10 3HS
Tel: 020 8442 2910; Travel: Highgate
Open: Mon-Sat 7.30am-9.30pm, Sun 11am-5pm

West

Eden Perfumes
PERFUMERIE
203 Portobello Road, W11 1LU
Tel: 077 9300 3413
www.edenperfumes.co.uk
Travel: Ladbroke Grove LU
Open: Mon 11am-6pm, Tues-Sat 10am-6pm, Sun 11am-5pm
Originally founded in Brighton, Eden Perfumes is a family-run vegan perfumery that has a smartly fitted out shop on Portobello Road. Using ingredients derived from vegetable products, they're able to replicate many favourite designer fragrances without any cruelty involved, which is an issue so ignored with larger name brands.

They also stock aftershaves, colognes and scented candles, meaning there's something for everyone at Eden Perfumes. Their fragrances are very affordable, costing only £18 and £24 for a 30ml and 50ml bottle respectively, making them far cheaper than the designer equivalent, though they are less glossily packaged. Eden offers samples and friendly service so customers can find exactly the perfume that's right for them. They are well worth a visit if you're in Portobello and also have an excellent website from where you can order for home delivery.

GreenBay
CRUELTY FREE SUPERMARKET
228 North End Road, W14 9NU
Tel: 020 7385 8913
www.greenbaysupermarket.co.uk
Travel: West Kensington LU
Open: Mon-Sat 10am-8pm, Sun 10am-6pm
London's first cruelty-free supermarket has joined a plethora
of plant-based eateries on North End Road and is just a few
doors down from the renowned 222 Vegan Cuisine (see p.145)
and a short walk from a branch of PickyWops (see p.146).
GreenBay may only be small, but it manages to cram in a wide
range of groceries, healthfoods and cosmetics and has over
a thousand products in its physical store, and plenty more
available via its website.

   GreenBay goes above and beyond to ensure that its stock
avoids animal products and is sourced from eco-friendly and
ethical suppliers. Here you'll find fresh groceries, 'cheezes',
milks and faux meats; dry foods like pulses, cereals, sauces
and spreads as well as household and health & beauty
products. Prices are slightly above the average, which is
understandable considering that they're operating on a much
smaller (yet still more ethical) scale. They also stock a great
deal of obscure and speciality products that will not only
make a vegan's life a lot easier, but also show omnivores
that nowadays everything you need can be plant based.
Though the larger retailers have begun to cater to the growing
demand for vegan products, GreenBay still stocks a far more
impressive variety of goods. If you can't make it to North End
Road their website is easy to use.

Hetu
VEGAN ZERO WASTE STORE
201 St. Johns Hill, SW11 1TH
Tel: 0739 170 0816
www.hetu.co.uk
Twitter/Insta: @hetu_uk
Travel: Clapham Junction LO and Rail
Open: Tues-Thurs 11am-7pm, Fri-Sun 11am-5pm

The future of retailing lies in shops like Hetu, which manages to supply an impressive range of vegan everyday and speciality products, all at affordable prices and with zero waste. From nut butters to cleaning products, Hetu have most things you need and are committed to providing sustainably sourced, unprocessed and unrefined foods. The shop might put ethics first, but it also pays a good deal of attention to aesthetics, creating an attractive place to do your shopping as can be seen on its active social media pages. Hopefully it won't be too long before shops like Hetu are popping up all over the place, but for now the denizens of Clapham can breathe a sigh of relief. Whether looking to do the weekly shop, or for more unusual products, Hetu have got you covered.

Organic for the People
VEGAN ORGANIC GROCERY STORE
29-30 High Street, W5 5DB
Tel: 020 3581 1080
Travel: Ealing Broadway
Open: Mon-Sat 8am-8pm, Sun 9am-6pm

It's all in the name, but just in case you hadn't twigged, this grocery store is an all-organic, all plant-based establishment that stocks an impressive range of products catering for vegans. Ranging from fresh fruit and veg, and dry goods, to chocolate treats and speciality 'health foods', they've got it all. The quality of the produce is high and they stock many of the leading vegan brands including Rainforest Foods, Rude Health and Bioitalia. The store is fairly large and an attractive place to shop with modern stainless steel shelving and white walls but has managed to keep everything at an affordable price range. The stock is clearly and cleanly laid out, but, as of yet, they don't have a chilled goods section. Organic for the People is a great shop, it's just a pity there aren't more stores like it in the capital.

Stella McCartney
CRUELTY FREE FASHION HOUSE

Brompton Cross, 91-95 Fulham Road, SW3 6RH
Tel: 020 7589 0092
www.stellamccartney.com
Twitter: @StellaMcCartney
Insta: @stellamccartney
Travel: South Kensington LU
Open: Mon-Sat 10am-6.30pm (Wed till 7pm), Sun 12noon-6pm

23 Old Bond Street, W1S 4PZ
Tel: 020 7518 3100
Travel: Green Park LU
Open: Mon-Sat 10am-6.30pm

One of the most prominent fashion brands in Britain, Stella McCartney is also one of the only high-end labels to have a vegetarian ethos. The label does use wool and silk but avoids leather and fur in its designs and offers many specifically vegan-friendly shoes and garments. The company pioneers ethical practices, including the use of synthetic wool and silk alternatives. The label offers Ready-To-Wear ranges primarily for women, with a more limited offering for men and children. Stella McCartney has concessions at some of the capital's large fashion retailers like Selfridges as well as two exquisitely designed London concept stores, which make for quite a shopping experience. Few good things come cheap, especially in the fashion world, and this label is very much at the high end of things. A simple t shirt starts from close to £200 and more elaborate dresses and outerwear sometimes cost upwards of £2000. Stella McCartney does however offer a more affordable line in collaboration with Adidas that is both stylish and sporty. These prices might be out of most people's budget but it's good to know there is a high-end vegetarian fashion label available for those that can afford it.

South

Fareshares

FOOD CO-OP AND COMMUNITY PROJECT
56 Crampton Street, SE17 3AE
www.fareshares.org.uk
Travel: Elephant and Castle LU
Open: Thurs 2pm-8pm, Fri 4pm-7pm, Sat 3pm-5pm

Fareshares is a food co-op in south London that has been making a concerted effort to provide affordable healthy food since the 90s. They stock all sorts of fresh fruit and veg, as well as dry goods like grains, nuts and pulses, all in bulk, so that it can be as cheap as possible. For those in need of bread, bottled goods and great organic produce, you need look no further. They've pioneered ways of reducing wastage by establishing a bring your own bag policy, and eliminating plastic packaging where possible. Nearly everything is organic, and they source locally where possible. This not for profit, volunteer-run community initiative is as good as it gets, and we encourage you to make a donation if visiting. It's only a pity that Fareshares is not open on more days, so when you do visit it's a good idea to stock up.

Well Being Sydenham
HEALTH FOOD SHOP
19 Sydenham Road, SE26 5EX
Tel: 020 8659 2003
Travel: Sydenham Rail
Open: Tues-Weds 9am-6.30pm,
Thurs-Sat 9am-6pm

Well Being is a health foods shop on Sydenham's busy high street that is a haven for local vegetarians, vegans and health conscious shoppers on the hunt for harder-to-find products. It has an impressive stock of health goods, ranging from organic peanut butter made by small co-operatives to muesli mixes, herbal remedies and quality chocolate. This great local store offers a wide range of products from established brands such as Jojoba skincare, Green & Black and Goodlife.

East

Dark Sugars
CHOCOLATIER

Dark Sugars Chocolates, 141 Brick Lane, E1 6SB
• Chocolate Shop, see page 294
Dark Sugars Cocoa House, 124-126 Brick Lane, E1 6RU
• Chocolate Café, see page 294

Fifth Dimension Tattoo and Piercing
VEGAN TATTOOIST AND PIERCING PARLOUR
16 Bacon Street, E1 6LF
Tel: 020 7613 2736
www.fifthdimensiontattoo.co.uk
Twitter: @5thDimension
Insta: @fifthdimensiontattoo
Travel: Shoreditch High Street LO/Liverpool Street LU
Open: Mon-Tues (appointment only),
Weds- Sat 11am-7pm, Sun 1pm-7pm
Operating as London's only vegan tattoo parlour, Fifth Dimension offers a range of styles from their three in-house artists. They have specialists on geometric and symbol tattoos, as well as new-school art and more classic watercolour work. Full body piercings are also available here and they sell a range of natural aftercare products for both services. Fifth Dimension is price competitive despite being in the heart of Shoreditch, with tattoos starting at £80 and piercings costing between £20 and £40 (each). Their work can be seen on their website and social media pages. Fifth Dimension is a welcome addition to the vegan businesses on Brick Lane.

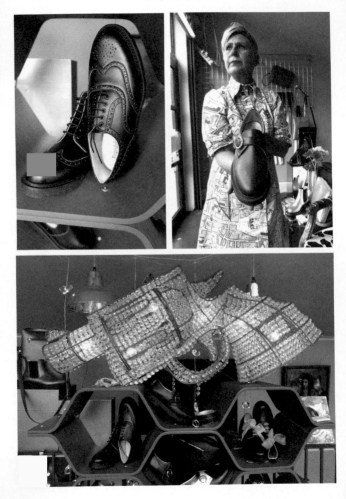

Friendship Shoes
CRUELTY FREE SHOEMAKER AND SHOP
272 Hackney Road, E2 7SJ
Tel: 020 7613 4265
www.friendship.shoes
Twitter: VeganShoesLon
Insta: friendshipveganshoes
Travel: Bethnal Green LU/Cambridge Heath LO
Twitter: @veganshoeslon/Insta: @friendshipveganshoes
Open: Tues-Sun 11am-8pm

Operating as both an online retailer and in-store boutique down the Hackney Road, Friendship Shoes produce vegan, non-leather shoes aimed at a more luxury market. Like the famous Northampton shoe producers, they utilise classic British engineering and design practices, such as the Goodyear welt, to deliver the same look and feel that should be expected from quality brogues, monk shoes and Chelsea boots.

As well as coming in classic blacks and browns, styles are also available in stunning silver and copper options. Their sizes run from UK size 3 right through to UK size 12, so men and women of whatever size and stature can find something here. A pair of Friendship's vegan shoes will set you back between £160 and £180, depending on the style, and if you want to try before you buy, you can do so from their showroom. They get the thumbs up from us and PETA too.

Grains and Greens
VEGAN GROCERY STORE
214 Mare Street, E8 3RD
Tel: 020 8985 6344
Travel: Hackney Central LO
Open: Daily 8am-9pm

This neighbourhood grocery store is a great option for your weekly vegan goods – it stocks everything from speciality faux meats to cleaning products, as well as whole foods. They're price competitive to other similar suppliers, and also have a small takeout service offering fresh foods like sandwiches. The store is narrow but surprisingly long with extensive shelving stocking all your vegan needs. A great vegan grocer that's well worth a try.

North

Earth Natural Foods
VEGETARIAN GROCERY STORE
200-202 Kentish Town Road, NW5 2AE
Tel: 020 7482 2211
www.earthnaturalfoods.co.uk
Travel: Kentish Town LU
Open: Mon-Sat- 8.30am-7pm, Sun 11am-5pm
Earth Natural Foods stocks only organic, vegetarian wholefoods and eco-friendly household goods, including all the essentials like seasonal fruit and veg, nuts and other dry goods, oils and lots of tempting sweet treats. You'll be able to get fresh sourdough breads, as well as free-from goods and takeaway salads here too. They're also taking a stand against plastic packaging, so bring your own reusable containers and top up on stock at discounted rate. They also carry many of the fair trade brands available and ethically produced health and beauty products.

Harmless

VEGAN PLASTIC FREE AND ZERO WASTE STORE

Blue House Yard, 5 River Park Road, N22 7TB
Tel: 0737 7322 426
www.harmlessstore.co.uk
Insta: @harmless_store
Travel: Wood Green LU
Open: Tues-Fri 11am-8pm, Sat 9.30am-4.30pm,
Sun 12noon-4:30pm

It's initiatives like Harmless that show vegan businesses to be at the forefront of reshaping consumer behaviour for the better. This is a vegan, plastic-free and zero-waste store that sells all the household essentials. Their spread of foodstuffs is extensive, with dry goods like pasta and pulses, dairy-free cheeses, chocolate treats and fresh fruits and veg too.

They sell cleaning, health and beauty products, and plenty of extras like water bottles and tote bags to help you keep your footprint as small as possible. Their goods adorn the walls in big glass containers and you pay by weight. This is a great way for north Londoners to reduce their plastic waste and help the environment – just don't forget to bring your own refillable containers.

The Third Estate
CRUELTY FREE CLOTHING STORE

27 Brecknock Road, London, N7 0BT
Tel: 020 3620 2361
www.thethirdestate.co.uk
Twitter: @thirdestate
Insta: @thethirdestatelondon
Travel: Kentish Town LU
Open: Tues 11am-7.30pm, Wed-Sat 10am-6pm

This clothing retailer operates both online and as an in-store boutique, from where it sells an entire range of casualwear for both men and women, including accessories like belts and bags, footwear and essentials like jackets and jeans. The overall aesthetic of their clothing is British normcore – the style is quiet and suitable for the everyday. You can expect to find a range of speciality vegan fashion lines, as well as some bigger name brands like Fred Perry.

With all of their stock The Third Estate ensure that not only do they never source anything that contains animal products, but also only work with suppliers that meet high social, labour and environmental standards, The Camden store is a little off the beaten track on Brecknock Road, but is well worth the effort with an extensive stock, great displays and helpful and friendly staff who are committed to the principles of cruelty-free living. If all this shopping has left you feeling peckish, the vegan eatery Healthy Wealthy is just opposite (see p.107).

Food Delivery Services

Vegan Apron

www.veganapron.com
Tel: 0800 634 2807
Twitter/Insta: @veganapron
This family-run firm is helping people on their vegan journey by delivering recipe cards and ingredients straight to your door. Boxes are priced between £31 and £41, and you can opt for boxes that contain a range of ingredients from soups and stews, to a large haul of fresh fruit and veg. This alternative to the weekly shop is a good way of bringing more wholefoods into your cooking. You'll be supporting organic farming practices too, as Vegan Apron work closely with farmers to ensure produce is always sustainable and seasonal. All produce is packed and delivered within 24 hours to ensure the ingredients arrive to you fresh. Boxes can be adjusted for dietary requirements.

Vegan Larder

Theveganlarder.com
Twitter/Insta:@vegan_larder
A sign of the changing times, Vegan Larder are the latest advent in services for plant-based eaters. They offer a food box delivery service in the UK on a subscription basis, which cost between £25 and £30. The contents of the boxes vary based on the seasons, but always include condiments like ketchup and balsamic dressing, and dry goods like fruit bars, crisps and crackers. Vegan Larder posts plenty of recipes online for all to enjoy, free of charge, that cover day-to-day cooking and less frequent treats like chocolate cakes. The team behind the business also provides kitchen consultancy to cafés, restaurants and caterers, helping them make the change to a plant-based menu, source better produce and market themselves more effectively.

Vegan Hair Salons

Some of London's hair salons have caught on to the turning tide and are swimming with the oncoming vegan wave, by only using products that are absolutely free from animal testing and products. You'll find these salons stretched out right across the capital, from Hackney to Hammersmith, so you won't have to travel far for an ethical haircut. They all offer the comprehensive services like cutting and colouring that you would expect, and some do more – at The Canary they've even got an amazing in-house vegetarian and vegan café. Muku are among the most well known, and offer premium services like 'Japanese straightening' and 'Brazilian Blowouts' across their three east London branches.

The salons are primarily female focused but do offer gents' cuts too. Our favourite has to be Glasshouse Salon – not only is the space one of the coolest in London, but the service they provide is second to none, which their Instagram can attest to. Like the others, they stock a plethora of fantastic hair and beauty products, which are available in store and online, which are well worth checking out for anyone looking for top-of-the-range cruelty free products.

The Canary

61-63 Old Bethnal Green Road, E2 6QA
Tel: 020 8257 8170
www.thecanary.co.uk
Insta: @thecanaryE2
Travel: Bethnal Green LU
Open: Wed-Fri 10am-8pm, Sat 10am-6pm, Sun 10am-5pm
for full review see p.249

Ena Salon

5 Great Queen Street, WC2B 5DG
www.enasalon.com
Insta: @enasalon
Tel: 020 3301 5451
Travel: Holborn LU
Open: Mon & Sat 9am-6pm, Tues 11am-8pm
Wed-Thurs 8.30am-9pm, Fri 9.30am-7pm

Glasshouse Salon

Netil House, 1 Westgate Street, E8 3RL
Tel: 020 3095 9783
www.glasshousesalon.co.uk
Insta: @glasshousejournal
Travel: Hackney Central/London Fields LO
Open: Tues 10am-8pm, Wed-Thu 11am-8pm
Fri 9am-6pm, Sat-Sun 10am-6pm

Monster House London

2 Heneage Street, E1 5LJ
Tel: 020 7377 6486
www.monsterhouselondon.co.uk
Travel: Aldgate East LU
Open: Mon-Sat 12noon-8pm

Muku Hair

www.mukuhair.com

DALSTON, 491-493 Kingsland Road, E8 4AU
Tel: 020 7249 8718
Insta: @mukuhair
Travel: Dalston Junction/Kingsland LO
Open: Tue-Fri 11am-8pm, Sat 11am-7pm, Sun 10am-5pm

SHOREDITCH, 109 Shoreditch High Street, E1 6JN
Tel: 020 7033 6520
Travel: Shoreditch High Street LO
Open: Mon-Fri 11am-8pm, Sat 11am-7pm, Sun 10am-5pm

SPITALFIELDS, 55 Commercial Street, E1 6BD
Tel: 020 7247 5732
Travel: Aldgate East/Liverpool Street LU/LO/Rail
Open: Tues-Fri 11am-8pm, Sat 11am-7pm,
Sun 10am-5pm

Rabbit Hole Hair Salon
49B Goldhawk Road, W12 8QP
Tel: 074 5022 5230
www.therabbitholelondon.com
Insta: @veganhairsalon
Travel: Goldhawk Road LU
Open: Mon-Fri 11am-7pm, Sat 10am-6pm, Sun 11am-5pm

Rococo Organic Salon
16 Webb's Road, SW11 1XJ
Tel: 074 6868 0000
www.rococo.salon
Insta: @rococosalon
Travel: Clapham South LU
Open: Mon-Sat 10am-8pm

Markets
& Events

Markets

Brixton Vegan Market

Brixton Station Road, SW9 8QQ
Twitter: @BrixtonVeganMkt
Insta: @brixtonveganmarket
Travel: Brixton LU
Open: Sun 11am-4pm June-Oct;
last Sun of the month Jan-March; Fortnightly April-May

This is a new market in Brixton that offers all kinds of vegan products and street food. It's a lot of fun and there is always great food from regular traders such as Sweet Tooth, Las Vegans and Picky Wops with new traders popping up every week. The market is run for the benefit of the local community and supports The People's Fridge and Brixton and Norwood Food Bank. There's no shelter on this traditional market street so the market only trades on a weekly basis in the summer months and less frequently during the rest of the year.

Broadway Vegan Market

Broadway Vegan Market

London Fields Primary School, Westgate Street, E8 3RU
www.thespreadfood.com
Twitter: @BroadwayVeganMK
Insta: @broadwayveganmarket
Travel: London Fields LO
Open: Sat 10am-4pm

This is the latest reincarnation of the Saturday market at London Fields Primary School. The new market is the brainchild of the people at The Spread, who run a number of food markets across London. Compared to your average market trader, the stall holders here are a cheerful and attractive advertisement for a plant based lifestyle, proferring samples aplenty and all of them willing to chat about their products and offer advice. Among this hardy band are Sam and Oli from Natural Born Wine with a carefully selected range of biodynamic wines and lots of info sheets for those who want to know more. Vegan cheese and nut spreads are available from the wittily named I Am Nut OK, while Nini Organics offer a range of vegan organic beauty products.

The rest of the market is dedicated to food with delicious vegan cakes provided by the likes of Lele's Café, Cakefully Heaven plus generous helpings of colourful vegan cakes from Bakings. For vegan food on the move, you won't be disappointed with vegan Sushi, hearty curries from Veeg, Vietnamese vegan food from Eat Chay and several stalls offering vegan takes on the traditional burger – among them The Green Grill. It's a pity that the market doesn't offer anything in the way of vegan ingredients to prepare your own food, but vegetables are not hard to find with Broadway Market just around the corner.

Hackney Downs Vegan Market

Hackney Downs Studios, Amhurst Terrace, E8 2BT
www.fatgayvegan.com
Twitter: @FatGayVegan
Insta: @fatgayvegan
Travel: Rectory Road, Hackney Downs, or Hackney Central LO
Open: Sat 11am-5pm

Vegan markets seem to be springing up all the time in London but Hackney Downs was the first on the scene and a template for much that has followed. Every Saturday the courtyard of Hackney Downs Studios hosts about 15 vegan street food traders and producers of vegan products.

There's a great choice of food from around the world with Bamboo Street Food offering a fusion of Shawarma Kebab, Burrito Samosas and Mexican Rice. The Big V London are regulars here and serve some of the best veggie burgers to be found in the capital. The team at Eat Chay dish up a great selection of plant-based Vietnamese food such as noodle salad and kimchi fried rice.

If you have a sweet tooth there are always a fair few specialists selling delicious vegan cupcakes, cookies and pastries. Completing the picture are a smattering of stalls selling vegan scented candles and Kinda Co. whose range of non-dairy spreads and deli products would grace any vegan's larder and Clarkshaws Brewery do a great line in vegan craft beer. The market is run by Sean O'Callaghan who blogs on all matters vegan under the nom de plume 'Fat Gay Vegan'. He does a good job of promoting the event and alternates stalls so that every week is slightly different. If the weather is bad and you don't fancy eating al fresco, Temple Goods (see p.138) is a comfy vegan eatery directly looking out onto the market.

Soho Vegan Market @Street Food Union

Rupert Street, W1D 6DS
www.streetfoodunion.com
Twitter: @sohoveganmarket
Travel: Leicester Square LU or Piccadilly Circus LU
Open: Sat 11am-4pm

Street Food Union run a street food market throughout the week on Rupert Street, but on Saturdays the emphasis is entirely on plant-based food from the likes of Jake's Vegan Steaks, Eat Chay and My Gulay. The market hosts around ten vegan street food specialists and although they get busy, there's plenty of outdoor seating to allow you to relax and enjoy your meal amid the hubbub of Soho.

Venn Street Market

Venn Street, Clapham, SW4 0AT
Twitter: @FatGayVegan
Insta: @fatgayvegan
Travel: Clapham Common LU
Open: Sat 10am-4pm

In September 2018 Sean O'Callaghan, AKA the Fat Gay Vegan, took over about a third of Clapham's long established food market, offering lots of great vegan street food and vegan products. It's a great opportunity for west London's vegans to enjoy the Hackney Downs vegan experience (see page 356) without the inconvenience of venturing east.

Events

Vegan Nights

Old Truman Brewery, 150 Brick Lane, E1 6QL
www.vegannights.uk
Twitter/ Insta: @vegannightsldn
Travel: Shoreditch High Street LO/Liverpool Street LU
Open: First Thursday of the month 5pm-11pm

This monthly night market is the place to be for London's vegans, but draws in many people waking up to the movement too. Set inside the Old Truman Brewery, stalls span the circumference of the area, showcasing the hottest cooking and entrepreneurship that the plant-based community has to offer. Whether you're after food, vegan products like t-shirts and skin care, or looking to attend a talk or yoga class, they've got you covered.

Weave your way through the crowds of trendies sprawled out across the faux lawn's comfy cushions and beanbags to try cuisine from all corners of the world. Get there early to avoid the queues of hungry punters who manage to eat all the food before the night is out. And for good reason – once you've tried King Cook's teriyaki chicken, or some of 90° MELT's dude food, you'll definitely be coming back. The healthy crowd can opt for Filipino salad boxes from Oh My Gulay while the indulgent can sample Black Milq's award winning ice creams. Regardless of what you eat, you'll be dancing it all off under the marquee, where the likes of BBC Radio 1Extra's Melody Kane smash out tunes for the revellers. With tickets for as little as £5-£7 and food the same, this is a top way to spend the first Thursday of the month.

Vegan Life Live London

Vegan Life Live London

Alexandra Palace, Alexandra Palace Way, N22 7AY

www.london.veganlifelive.com

Twitter: @veganlifelive

Insta: @veganlife_live

Travel: Alexandra Palace Rail,

Wood Green LU (then free shuttle bus)

Every February or March

This annual event is a festival of everything vegan with cookery demonstrations, ethical clothing, cruelty-free cosmetics, live performances and Q&A's with experts in plant-based living. Vegan Life is an event where you can spend a day milling around discovering new products and ideas and if you feel peckish there's a food court where some of the best vegan street food can be tried, from veggie burgers to substantial Indian curries. The event is always well attended so be prepared for some queueing, but the wait is worth it and chances are once you've visited you'll come back for more.

PlantBased Live

www.plantbasedlive.com

Excel, London, E16 1XL

Travel: Custom House DLR

Annual event in September

The team behind PlantBased magazine have launched this two day event dedicated to exploring the potential of a vegan life style with cookery demonstrations, cruelty-free free products, expert advice, demonstrations and much more. If watching all the cookery demonstrations leaves you feeling peckish, there is also a food court with fantastic vegan street food from around the globe, from falafels to faux fish and chips.

Mildred's King's Cross

Index

Index

Index

Index

Image Credits

KATAKATA

About us:

Metro is a small independent publishing company with a reputation for producing well-researched and beautifully-designed guides on many aspects of London life.

In fields of interest as diverse as shopping, bargain hunting, architecture, the arts, and food, our guide books contain special tips you won't find anywhere else.

www.metropublications.com

London's Hidden Walks Series

LONDON'S HIDDEN WALKS
THE LONDON WE KNOW IS JUST THE SURFACE!
Volume 1

LONDON'S HIDDEN WALKS
EXPLORE LONDON AND DISCOVER HOW 2000 YEARS OF HISTORY HAVE SHAPED THIS CITY
Volume 2

LONDON'S HIDDEN WALKS
WALK, EXPLORE, DISCOVER...
Volume 3

LONDON'S MARKETS
IN THE CANAL-LINED STREET-MARKETS OF HOCK-FARS, GARAGE-LANDS & CAPITOL SALES

LONDON'S HOUSES
FROM WORKHOUSE TO ROYAL PALACE, COME IN, CLOSE THE DOOR AND STEP BACK IN TIME...

LONDON'S MONUMENTS
FROM BOUDICCA AND BYRON TO GUY THE GORILLA

LONDON'S PARKS AND GARDENS
COVER MORE THAN TWENTY-FIVE PERCENT OF THE CAPITAL – THAT'S A LOT MORE GRASS BETWEEN TOES THAN ANY OTHER CITY IN EUROPE

LONDON'S CEMETERIES
SPEND THE DAY WITH KARL MARX, ENID BLYTON, KEITH MOON AND MANY MORE

EDINBURGH'S HIDDEN WALKS
WALK, EXPLORE, DISCOVER...